The Hanged Man and the Body Thief

The Hanged Man and the Body Thief

Finding Lives in a Museum Mystery

ALEXANDRA ROGINSKI

Monash University Publishing
Matheson Library and Information Services Building
40 Exhibition Walk
Monash University
Clayton, Victoria 3800, Australia
www.publishing.monash.edu

Monash University Publishing brings to the world publications which advance the best traditions of humane and enlightened thought. Monash University Publishing titles pass through a rigorous process of independent peer review.

http://publishing.monash.edu/books/hmbt-9781922235664.html

Series: Australian History
Design: Les Thomas

National Library of Australia Cataloguing-in-Publication entry

Creator:	Roginski, Alexandra, author
Title:	The Hanged Man and the Body Thief: Finding Lives in a Museum Mystery
ISBN:	9781922235664
Subjects:	Crow, Jim--Death and burial.
	Hamilton, A. S.
	Museum Victoria.
	Aboriginal Australians--Biography.
	Phrenology--Australia--History.
	Body snatching--Australia.
Dewey Number:	920.00929915

Printed in Australia by Griffin Press an Accredited ISO AS/NZS 14001:2004 Environmental Management System printer.

Contents

About the Author

Alexandra Roginski lives in Canberra, where she is a doctoral candidate researching the history of popular phrenology at the Australian National University. Originally from Melbourne, she has written for *The Age*, the *Big Issue*, and specialist publications in education, research and development. Her interest in the history of science developed during a period when she was working in medical communications. In 2013, Alexandra was awarded an 1854 Student Scholarship from Museum Victoria, where she has also worked as a research assistant in Indigenous repatriation. This is her first book.

Prologue

It was March when I first held the manila folder that would set me on the trail of two dead men. At the time, I was in a narrow, brightly lit research room in the Humanities Department of Museum Victoria, digging through old letter files related to a relationship that was established between the Museum and Victoria Police in 1902 for the procurement of Aboriginal remains.[1] One of my Museum contacts had asked me to familiarise myself with this manila folder, which contained clues to the identity of an executed Aboriginal man, in case I came across him in my research.

The file dated back to the 1980s, when the Museum began to repatriate its extensive collection of human remains (mostly Aboriginal), and related to a skull that had persistently baffled researchers.[2] It was part of a collection of about 55 skulls and skull fragments gathered by the nineteenth-century phrenologist AS Hamilton, and its deteriorated label read simply: 'Jim Crow, Aboriginal ... executed ... land ... capital offences'. The edges of the folder were softened by decades-worth of fingers fossicking through the hand-written, typed and printed notes it contained. In order for this skull to be repatriated, the origins and cultural affiliation of the remains had to be known. But rather than pinpointing just one man with this name, the file contained an identity parade of Jim Crows from across Victoria. The question seemed almost not *Who was Jim Crow?* but *Who wasn't?*

Considering the history of the search, it seemed unlikely that I would stumble across any documentation related to this person in my work. Nevertheless, I decided to tick off a few basics. I opened Google and typed in the search terms 'Jim Crow' and 'AS Hamilton'. The result was almost instantaneous: a link to an 1862 newspaper report from the Brisbane *Courier*. It detailed a phrenological lecture in which Hamilton had demonstrated his craft using the skull of an Aboriginal man named Jim Crow, executed at Maitland in 1860 for raping a European woman.[3] Digitised through the National Library of Australia's Trove database, the article established a provenance for Jim Crow, not in Victoria, and specifically not in Portland, as previous researchers had speculated when wrestling with the barely legible place name on the label, but in New South Wales.

Technology had opened a new avenue of enquiry into a 30-year mystery. But, at the tail end of a scorching summer, my search for Jim Crow was only just beginning.

A researcher, a Scotsman and Crow

After countless heartbeats, breaths and muscular twitches of the great human machine, a person can be dissected and their skull removed. A label may be pasted onto the side of this skull, or a circular portion of bone the size of a 20-cent coin excised for scientific reasons at which we can only guess. At some point, this divided person may be sold or gifted among other chattels. These are the cold logistics of how Jim Crow became a museum object, a silent slate onto which Hamilton and subsequent owners could project whatever version of Aboriginality they deemed fit.

The process of seeking provenance for Aboriginal remains is about resurrecting the subject from the museum piece so that he or she can go home to country. Repatriation expert Michael Pickering, Head of the Aboriginal and Torres Strait Islander Program at the National Museum of Australia, posits that the key question for historians working with remains should be 'Where are the Stories?':

> We have a responsibility to document these stories, in all of their manifestations ... The passing of time filters out the

horrors, emotions, and the social impacts until ultimately we
are left with the institutional and professional objectification
of life and death. Everything is neat, clean, tidy, and boxed.[4]

This book provides a case study of this process of finding the stories.
Its driving goal has been to source enough information on the life
and death of Jim Crow to enable his return to country, which we
now know is situated on the central coast of New South Wales.

The story spans a century and a half, moving back and forth over
the decades.

Aboriginal concepts of time are radically different to those of
Europeans, with attachments to ancestors and spirits that have
contemporary implications observed throughout the continent.
This alternate understanding of time is compounded in the context
of the transgenerational impacts of colonisation. Aboriginal health
researcher Judy Atkinson explains how traumas play out at a community level:

> The fabric and soul of relations and beliefs in and about
> people fragments and fractures. The intricate web of relations
> that binds people together no longer holds. People lose the
> knowledge of who they are, and they no longer know life
> as meaningful ... Without purpose, the past-present-future
> becomes weighted down with question marks.[5]

As will be discussed in this work, repatriation can play a role in not
only attempting to heal past wounds inflicted to the memory of the
person collected and to their kin, but also in opening new pathways
towards healing for the entire community.

Chapter One, 'Reassembling', is the contemporary piece of
the puzzle. It outlines the history and guiding principles of the
repatriation movement that inspired me to pursue this research at
the Museum Victoria, as well as discussing the practical aspects of
such work. The ubiquity of the name Jim Crow was the first major

obstruction in the process of establishing its provenance, but the shadow hanging over the project for most of the year was a question of the skull's sex, which had earlier been determined as female. I attempted to reconcile this impasse through a combination of historical speculation and theoretical gymnastics until, ultimately, the resolution came through a reassessment of the remains.

Chapters Two and Three reconstruct the respective lives of Jim Crow and phrenologist Archibald Sillars Hamilton. Although this thesis seeks to be an Aboriginal history in the sense of focusing on Aboriginal people, the two men have been twined together; they demand to be considered in tandem. In his seminal work *Hunters and Collectors*, historian Tom Griffiths describes how an eel net acquired in 1902 that is today part of collections at Museum Victoria served as a model from which the late Aboriginal elder Connie Hart could learn how to make such traditional nets in the late twentieth century.[6] The relationship of Jim Crow and Hamilton offers a grim parallel. It is only because Hamilton collected Jim Crow that we consider his life and alleged crimes here in any depth. Conversely, Hamilton's infamy and success were the sum of the people in his collection. They are two sides of the one coin, particularly when we start to consider their contrasting experiences of the colonial legal system.

There remains little information on the first 20 or so years of Jim Crow's life, and he first appears in the documentary record as part of the criminal prosecution that led to his death. Chapter Two, 'A Life Found in Death', works backwards from execution to find an entry point to understanding this young man. Using documentary sources – local histories, lists of the names of Aboriginal people prepared for the New South Wales Colonial Secretary's Office, ethnological texts – and the works of historians such as Henry Reynolds, I seek to identify the group to which Jim Crow may have belonged, and to speculate on the kind of world he inhabited on the margins of this new society. I then examine the events surrounding the alleged rape for which he was executed, as well as his committal hearing and trial. In light of outcomes from several other sexual offence trials heard around the same time, I ask this fundamental question: Would Jim Crow have been convicted and executed were he not Aboriginal?

While Crow awaited his end, travelling phrenologist Hamilton was already attracting headlines in the Maitland area with popular lectures that featured real human skulls. Using these, he illustrated the claims of this influential practice: that character and morality could be judged from the shape of a person's head. Like a fly drawn to fresh meat, Hamilton attended Jim Crow's execution. But it was his attempt four months later to have Jim Crow's head exhumed from its grave, and the ensuing prosecution of the grave-robbing phrenologist, that captured the attention of newspapers around Australia. After setting the scene for the nineteenth-century fascination with human remains, Chapter Three, 'Scottish Head Case', discusses Hamilton's exhumation trial and takes a broader view of his tumultuous career. What motivated Hamilton in his collecting? Did he truly believe that phrenology could delineate character and intellect? Or was this discipline simply a dramatic way for him to make a living?

To study the history of this period is to be confronted by a disparity between the amounts of European and Aboriginal written sources, as the Aboriginal record was most often only an oral one. Historian Bain Attwood articulates this tension when describing how historians of the frontier "have to rely on texts created by white people. We never have Aboriginal voices unless whites recount (and invariably reformulate) these in their writings".[7] Here, Crow's voice is heard only in one brief statement made during committal proceedings, while that of Hamilton resonates through countless newspaper articles and several prolix pamphlets. The challenge of dealing with loud historical figures such as Hamilton is that, no matter how gruesome their behaviour, we start to warm to the very humanity of their voice. Far from breeding contempt, familiarity can also breed comfort. It is an ambivalence that historians often experience when studying the works of figures such as George Augustus Robinson. As leader of the 'Friendly Mission' in Tasmania that aimed to find and contain the remaining few-hundred Aboriginal people on the island, and later, as Chief Protector of Aborigines in the Port Phillip District (soon to become the new colony of Victoria), Robinson personifies the paternalism of Colonial rule; but as an assiduous documenter, his account also forms a backbone to Aboriginal history from these regions. This book engages with these tensions by frequently interrogating the context of sources, particularly as they relate to the criminal proceedings around Jim Crow's conviction.

Long after Hamilton died in 1884, Jim Crow would continue to pass through the hands of anatomists and physical anthropologists, researchers applying new sciences of the twentieth century to understanding the enduring question of human form. Chapter Four, 'Mrs Hamilton Presents a Collection', discusses the gifting of the remains in 1889 by his third wife, Agnes Hamilton, who packed the skulls and sent them south along the east coast of Australia on a steamer. I will describe how the collection's resting place was determined by the scientific interests and politics of the powerful Board of Trustees of the Public Library, Museums, and National Gallery of Victoria, and by the charismatic museum directors. While Hamilton's widow may have intended the collection to memorialise the phrenologist's life work, the reality of the collection's division at the museum meant that Hamilton's identity as collector became as distorted over subsequent decades as those of his skulls.

Today we look sternly on the macabre aspects of nineteenth-century phrenology. But in Chapter Four, I raise the possibility that, even in 1889, Hamilton's track record of exhumation and his strident political activism in the case of Ned Kelly contributed to the Board of Trustees suppressing the collection's arrival at the museum. Hamilton was never truly respectable in any period. This feeling grows when one handles his collection, seeking clues to the disturbed remains of people sentenced to disintegration in boxes. In some of the skulls, the soil and sand that colonise the interstices between facial bones speak of the country from which they were wrested.

This book cannot explain where the rest of Jim Crow's remains may be, or answer the question of what will happen to his skull. That will be for the relevant Aboriginal groups to determine. But it presents the evidence and stories necessary for that decision-making process to begin, a conversation that the Museum Victoria repatriation team are now holding with groups from the region of Jim Crow's birth.

Ultimately, the story will never be complete, but perhaps that is fitting; Crow himself is fragmented. We do not know whether the rest of him was also exhumed by Hamilton, or if his postcranial remains are still in the St Peter's Church of England Cemetery in East Maitland. I visited this place in the distant hope that somehow it might yield answers, following a muddy path through vacant council land to a windy hill from which gravestones poked like ragged teeth. But the cemetery is derelict. Trees and rabbit warrens have tumbled headstones, tall grasses hiding snakes and secrets. A sign at the main gate states a prohibition on digging around the graves, yet the vandalism that has left family crypts broken open or collapsed is oddly sympathetic to history: Hamilton desecrated graves here more than 150 years ago.

Chapter One

Reassembling

Jim Crow's death certificate plays an ironic role in this investigation. Marking the end of his life, it is also the only document bearing information of his birth in Clarence Town, a small locality near the regional hub of Maitland, information crucial for identifying which Aboriginal group should be approached regarding his remains.[1]

Yet, as a product of the colonial bureaucracy, the certificate does not divulge Jim Crow's Aboriginal name, how he came to be called Jim Crow, or his cultural affiliation (the last of which is not necessarily tied to birthplace or habitation, and which will be discussed further in Chapter Two). As such, the certificate could be seen as characteristic of much of this search, in which fresh answers were always somehow outweighed by the new questions springing up alongside them. The common name Jim Crow, which I will discuss in this chapter, was a major sticking point in solving the skull's identity. But there was another dramatic complication: in recent decades, the remains had been repeatedly identified as female.[2]

This chapter begins by discussing the recent history of repatriation, and presents a case study of a particularly complicated investigation. It explains the problem-solving approach that this project demanded, an approach that embraced physical anthropology, museology and even the science of sex differentiation.

The great return

Since the 1980s, all major museums in Australia and many around the world have developed partnerships with Indigenous communities that include, among their purposes, the return of culturally sensitive collections. These collections largely comprise human remains and are stored under restricted conditions, with viewing limited to individuals granted permission through a rigorous Indigenous advisory process.[3] Within museum walls, these remains exist in a liminal space in which their human history is at conflict with the labelling, boxing and general ownership that marks their transformation to objecthood.[4] To repatriate human remains is therefore not only to remove them from the museum, but also to attempt to remove the museum from *within them*, stripping away institutional context and ownership to allow a rehabilitation of the subject.

The National Museum of Victoria, as it was known from the heady days of Gold Rush-era Melbourne until 1984, became a major collecting point for human remains at the beginning of the twentieth century, and continued to officially accumulate remains until a landmark event in the mid 1980s dramatically changed its practices.[5] The events of that year hinged on a collection of remains exhumed between the 1930s and 1950s from sites along the Murray River by George Murray Black, civil engineer, Gippsland landowner and amateur excavator of bodies.[6] Black had collected the remains of up to 1800 Aboriginal people, with about 800 of them ending up in the Department of Anatomy at the University of Melbourne.[7] In 1986, at the instigation of Museum employee Jim Berg, and following several high-profile heritage cases, the Victorian Aboriginal Legal Service took action against the University for the surrender of the remains.[8] The University argued that science would suffer if the remains were removed, but the Supreme Court of Victoria ultimately ordered the collection to be sent to Museum Victoria, where steps would be taken towards its repatriation.[9]

The Murray Black case became one of the first major repatriation cases in Australia, and the process of sorting the collection – which had been aggregated as femurs, crania and sundry other bones types

– in order to reassemble the individuals also triggered a review of the other human remains in the Museum's collections. But the tides had already been turning for some decades. Repatriation scholar Cressida Fforde traces the movement to the 1960s, when Indigenous groups began claiming rights to remains stored in museums and collections.[10] In 1978, A UNESCO regional seminar hosted in Adelaide recommended that museums foster new relationships and working practices to connect them to the Indigenous communities from which collections were sourced.[11] In the US, 1990 saw the passage of the national Native American Graves Protection and Repatriation Act (although various states had already been repatriating remains since the 1980s).[12] That same year, across the Atlantic, the University of Edinburgh medical school, laden with the legacy of a grisly collecting history, began taking steps to repatriate Tasmanian Aboriginal remains to the National Museum in Canberra.[13] In 1993, the goals of returning remains and forging partnerships with Indigenous people were articulated by the Council of Australian Museum Associations (as the peak body was known) in *Previous Possessions, New Obligations: Policies for Museums in Australia and Aboriginal and Torres Strait Islander People*, a document replaced in 2005 by *Continuous Cultures, Ongoing Responsibilities*.

Since then, an increasing number of institutions in Europe, America and Australia have returned Aboriginal remains, although many still retain collections. In 2013, for example, remains collected by anthropologist Eric Mjöberg in 1910 were returned by the Swedish government to the Nyikina Mangala community of the Kimberley.[14] Physical anthropologists continue to work with Aboriginal remains, although they today do so only with the consent and partnership of Aboriginal communities.[15]

Repatriation can be a protracted process. For example, cultural historian Martin Thomas describes how the return of ancestral remains from the Smithsonian Institution to an Arnhem Land community took "about a decade from the late 1990s, involved lobbying at an intergovernmental level, and provoked enormous hostility from certain factions at the Smithsonian, particularly within the National Museum of Natural History, an institution deeply divided about the status of its large transnational collection of human remains".[16] Even once Indigenous groups have accepted responsibility for particular remains, they may still ask Australian museums to house them indefinitely if they are unable to arrange immediate burial. In line with the policies in *Continuous Cultures, Ongoing Responsibilities*, the museum is then obliged to "abide by any reasonable conditions sought by those custodians".[17] And those remains that are difficult to provenance, such as many of the skulls in the Hamilton Collection, may wait decades before beginning their final journey.

A chance to heal

Funerary practices and burial sites that pay the requisite level of respect to the bodies of departed loved ones are central to most cultures. For proof of this point, we need only consider the cases of six Australian servicemen killed while on duty in Vietnam who were repatriated between 2007 and 2009.[18]

But for Aboriginal groups, the experience of being confronted by their "Old People" within museum settings is far more common than for the general Australian public. The pain that this can cause is reflected by Jim Berg in his account of first seeing the Murray Black remains at the University of Melbourne:

> Inside the cabinets there were rows and rows of the Skeletal Remains of Our Ancestors. We saw the numbers on each bone... We saw the empty eye sockets of rows and rows of skulls looking at us; I felt very emotional, very tearful and very disturbed as I looked into those empty eye sockets... When we [Berg and his wife] were alone, I looked at my

Ancestors and I said: "I am going to make sure that you all are going home to your Country."[19]

This anecdote captures one of the driving arguments for repatriation: respectful and appropriate burial, which many Aboriginal people believe to be crucial for the spirit journey of the deceased.[20]

By undoing the objectification of the Aboriginal body so emblematic of colonial oppression, repatriation can also play an important restorative role in many Aboriginal communities, becoming what Shannon Faulkhead and Jim Berg describe as an act of decolonisation.[21] In some cases, these healing effects can include the revival of old reburial ceremonies, or the creation of new ones, through a contemporary understanding of past practices. For example, the potential for strengthening the community is evidenced in the case of Tambo, a Manbarra man from Palm Island who travelled overseas as part of a circus in 1883 and died in Ohio in 1884.[22] As explained by Walter Palm Island, Manbarra elder, Tambo's repatriation from the US in 1993 provided an opportunity to revive a burial ceremony that had not been practised for many years, and the resulting festivities also created a point of celebration and identity not only for Palm Island's autochthonous Manbarra, but also for the Bwgaman, descendants of Aboriginal people brought there during the colonial period.[23]

Jim Crow jumps continents

In today's social imagination, the name Jim Crow often evokes the US civil rights movement and the 'Jim Crow laws' that represented systematised racial discrimination. But, during the nineteenth century, Jim Crow was also a common name for Aboriginal men. Notably, a Victorian Aboriginal man named Lyterjebillijun or 'Jim Crow' was part of the Aboriginal cricket team that travelled to

London in 1868.[24] Jim Crow also served as a nickname for Mount Franklin Station, situated on Dja Dja Wurrung country in central Victoria, and was the name bestowed on a goldfield in the region (the squatters of the area referred to Mount Franklin as 'Jim Crow Hill').[25]

This popularity raises valuable questions about the processes by which Aboriginal people acquired English names during this period. The name itself stems from 'Jump Jim Crow', a minstrel song that was first staged in 1828 and which was seminal to the genre that relied on caricatures depicting 'dim-witted' plantation Negros.[26] The song became an international sensation, and newspaper articles tell us that during Jim Crow's lifetime the name was also bestowed on a racehorse and a ship, and was used as an alias by European criminals.[27] Imagery of the 'American negro' was familiar in the Australian colonies: the Maitland Black Boy, a hitching post from the United States, has been a feature of the Maitland streetscape since 1866; a carving of a stereotypically jolly 'plantation negro' is displayed in Narynna, a heritage house in Hobart, Tasmania.[28] What's more, some former African American slaves actually ended up in the Antipodes, with Cassandra Pybus documenting cases of individuals who escaped from the US to England during the War of Independence, only to be later transported to Australia as convicts.[29] The name Jim Crow, transferred to Australian Aboriginal people, therefore not only served to trivialise identity by referencing a musical joke, but also submerged Aboriginal people into a homogenous blackness with African American slaves.

The triviality of the name accords with monikers for Aboriginal men such as Blackboy, Tom Jones and Time of Day, which appear in the 1837 New South Wales blanket registers for Dungog, a town situated 23 kilometres north of Clarence Town on the Williams River (for many years Clarence Town was part of the Dungog District).[30] This trivialisation can also be inferred from the repetition of many common first names in these lists. For example, the 54 Aboriginal men listed in 1837 include five men named Jemmy, four named Jackey or Jackie, and three named Billy. Several of the Jemmys, Jackies and Billys are numbered to differentiate them.

However, we should not simply assume that these naming practices represent an absolute imbalance of power. Historian Marilyn Wood suggests that the acquisition of European names, at least in the early days of settlement, was part of an intercultural negotiation between Aboriginal people and settlers, "characterised by active and reflexive attempts on both sides to understand and incorporate the other into their respective social schemas".[31] The inclusion of Aboriginal names (at least for the men) in the Dungog blanket registers of 1837, 1838 and 1842 indicates that Aboriginal identities were recognised by European authorities within this region around the time of Jim Crow's birth and childhood.[32] Furthermore, we do not know in every case whether the English names were adopted by Aboriginal people or bestowed upon them.[33] And even if these names *were* given by the person who listed recipients, in this case the police magistrate, the repetition and oddness of names could reflect the scribe's own frustration at having to give European names in order to work to the template required by the Colonial Secretary's Office, when Aboriginal names were readily available.[34]

It is also worth considering that those Aboriginal men who adopted the name Jim Crow may not necessarily have seen the minstrel character as a racial joke, but perhaps as a famous figure memorialised with his own song. The name may have in fact connected to their own social structure. The kinship system of most Aboriginal groups is based around moieties – two primary groups into which the community is divided. These two groups intermarry, while marriage between two members of the same moiety is prohibited. In his 1889 book, *Eaglehawk and Crow*, Presbyterian minister and ethnographer John Mathew documented the prevalence of these birds for designating moiety in Victoria and, to a lesser degree, in New South Wales and South Australia.[35] The name Jim Crow might therefore have been a way for Aboriginal people to preserve their traditional kinship classifications when adopting the European system of personal naming (in a parallel example, contemporary cultural historian Martin Thomas has noted how in north-western New South Wales the section name 'Kubbi' became "a well-known Aboriginal surname").[36] But regardless of these possible intentions, the minstrel connotations could only serve within the developing social systems of settler society to reinforce the subordinate status of its bearer.[37] The name also enabled the administrative erosion of Jim Crow's Aboriginal identity, with his other name not appearing in depositions from his committal proceedings, in court reporting, or on his death certificate. When he stepped up to the scaffold, Jim Crow was a man with a European name derived from an African American character played by a white man. And his tribal identity had become every bit as generalised as his name, referred to simply as 'Aboriginal'.

A matter of sex

The question of the name was answered through research into its minstrel origins, but conflicting information about the sex of the skull for a long time created uncertainty about Jim Crow's identity.

The distinction commonly used to differentiate between male and female skulls was explained by physical anthropologist John Lundy in 1981:

> As the female progresses … into adulthood, her skull retains many of the prepubertal traits, such as smoothness and gracility. The male on the other hand has a skull which exhibits more robusticity with larger muscle attachment areas such as crests and tuberosities, more pronounced brow ridges and the like.[38]

Other skeletal elements are of course also used to judge sex, with the most useful being the pelvis. Because of the physical diversity among population groups, experts establish the spectrum of maleness through to femaleness within a particular racial group based on measurements of a sample of remains.[39] The determination by physical anthropologist Colin Pardoe that the skull marked Jim Crow was female was based on overall morphology, incorporating measures such as the spectrum from gracility to robusticity. It was also based on the technique of biometric analysis, which compares size and shape within and between groups.[40]

Canadian-born Pardoe is a pioneer of a collaborative approach to archaeology that recognises "Indigenous control over their heritage, including the bodies of their ancestors".[41] He has also assessed the likely provenance of hundreds of Aboriginal remains in Australian museums, working from a large database of biometrics that he has compiled from collections in Australia and around the world. This method, which he terms a 'Remains Identification Program', has helped to establish the likely provenance of many ancestral remains, allowing for their return to relevant Aboriginal groups.[42]

As a result of Pardoe's determination that the skull labelled 'Jim Crow' was female, it was speculated that the skull could be that of an unidentified woman from the Dja Dja Wurrung group, many of who had lived at the station also known as Jim Crow. This explanation seemed even more feasible considering the predominance of Victorian remains housed at Museum Victoria. The Dja Dja Wurrung were approached by the Museum's repatriation team, and agreed to take possession of the skull. But these steps were halted when historical information emerged suggesting a provenance in coastal New South Wales.

I considered three possibilities when thinking about the conundrum of the skull's sex: the assessment that this person was female was an error arising from the ambiguities inherent to sexing in physical anthropology; Crow, outwardly male, had a developmental condition that rendered his skull uncharacteristically female; or a mix-up had occurred, the label was attached to the wrong skull, and this was not the skull of Jim Crow at all.

Pardoe himself explains some of the difficulties of sex determination in a recent report conducted for another Australian state museum.

> Sex of the individual skeleton can be determined with a good degree of accuracy. There is, however, considerable overlap in size between the sexes. This is common among many animals, and humans consistently have a large degree of overlap, regardless of the size of the population … A small number of cases will be misidentified.[43]

Sex determination becomes more difficult when isolated parts of the skeleton are used, in this case the skull. Paleoanthropologist Peter Brown pointed out in a 1981 paper that because of intrinsic human variation, "it is unlikely that any method of sex determination based on isolated bones of the human skeleton, including the pelvis, will ever achieve a resolution greater than 85–90 [per cent]".[44] Brown trialled an improved sexing method using a sample of remains from the Murray Black collection,[45] but found that, at best, 94.3 per cent of the female skulls could be correctly sexed, and 89.4 per cent of the male skulls.[46]

A reading that divides men and women into two distinct categories also excludes people who are intersex and possess attributes of both a man and woman or not enough of either to be normatively classed as male or female.[47] Considering that the occurrence of intersex within the population is medically documented (although its frequency is variously argued as ranging from 0.018 per cent to 2 per cent of live births), we could speculate that Jim Crow had a condition that resulted in his having a 'female' skull.[48] If intersex conditions can cause dramatic gonadal differences, could they impact on the skeleton of someone living a 'male' life, rendering skeletal traits feminine?

Another possibility was that Jim Crow's name was intentionally attached to a female skull, either by Hamilton or one of his agents. Based on the phrenologist's questionable moral fibre (to be discussed in Chapter Three), one could imagine that he may have viewed his failure to obtain the skull as a personal shortcoming; could he have knowingly mislabelled the skull of a woman as Jim Crow to fill this absence in his collection? Equally, if Hamilton had paid somebody else to retrieve the skull, this person may have fooled him as to its identity.

It is also possible that subsequent custodians mislabelled the collection. A 20-year gap divides Hamilton's death in 1884 and the collection's registration at the Museum in the early 1900s (we know that he continued to lecture with his collection until close to his death). This provides a large window of time in which anatomists or pseudo-scientists could have attached their own labels to the skulls in the Hamilton collection, possibly making a fundamental error of identity.

Male to female and back to male

In August 2013, when the list of possibilities for the skull's sex threatened to become more hindrance than help, a physical anthropological *deus ex machina* resolved the vexing question.

The Museum engaged Pardoe to reassess the remains, and although his measurements of the skull yielded the same data as in his first assessment, the proven historical link with Hamilton meant that these measurements were now considered in a different light.[49] But even with this new documentary information about where Jim Crow came from, Pardoe wrote that the skull's dimensions still produced ambiguous results within the sample he uses for biometric provenancing: the skull "grouped with the NSW coast with one set of variables and grouping criteria, but also with the Northern Territory and Victoria south of the Murray River". Despite being probably "south-eastern in affiliation, the result is inconclusive", he reported. He has since explained to me that this task was made more complicated because he was assessing Crow's skull against those of *males* from these particular groupings, and this was a highly uncharacteristic male skull. In the report, Pardoe posited that the reliability of provenancing would have been affected if Jim Crow perhaps had a European parent. Furthermore, the man's stature, gauged upon his admission to Maitland Gaol as being 5'1½", with his build listed as 'slight', may also have contributed to the inconclusive nature of the results. [50] Pardoe concluded that the archival materials were "strong and persuasive" and that the "small size, question of sex, and possible European ancestry cannot be reconciled by reference to skeletal investigation".[51] With physical anthropology unable to untangle these complications, he wrote, the historical record should be preferred. The skull marked Jim Crow was male.

Reassembling

Although the story of the Hamilton collection's journey to the Museum remains imperfect, the resolution of the sex issue meant that research into the life of Jim Crow could now focus on questions such as his cultural affiliation, a matter central to his possible repatriation. Jim Crow had spent more than a century in the collections of Museum Victoria, but we could start to build the picture of him as a man, breathing life into the skull to try to make him a human being again.

Chapter Two

A Life Found in Death

26 April 1860

On an April morning within the sandstone walls of the Maitland Gaol, a slight Aboriginal man wearing a white shirt and light trousers was led from the cell that had been his home for almost three months.[1]

Jim Crow had spent most of his 25 or so years within 50 kilometres of Maitland, the thriving colonial city and river port that was the locus for the settled districts north of Sydney. Although he never travelled far (to our present-day knowledge), this young Aboriginal man had lived and breathed in a terrain of green pasture, mountain-edged horizons and wide, sumptuous rivers. During his lifetime, access to land by the Aboriginal groups in this landscape had shrunken irrevocably, a compression symbolised by Jim Crow's own final transition to incarceration. Upon leaving his cell on this morning with his arms pinioned, Crow saw the sky and felt cool autumnal air on his skin. But the sensation was brief, a condemned man's freedom.

Just one month before, Jim Crow had been sentenced to "the extreme penalty of the law" after a jury of white men found him guilty of rape. Fifty or sixty people were now assembled in the gaolyard to watch his execution alongside that of convicted murderer John Jones.[2]

The colonial newspaper *Empire* reported that the day's business took place with "decency and order". Jones cast off his shoes and ascended the scaffold first, Crow following. While white caps were pulled over their heads and nooses placed around their necks, the Anglican Reverend John Albert Greaves read a final service.

Prayer concluded. The executioner pulled the lever and a clang resonated through the yard as the platform fell out from beneath the condemned men's feet. The end was quick for Jones; Jim Crow struggled longer. But both were dead within moments.[3]

Jim Crow left few clues to his short life. The most information we can gather emerges from the parsimonious documentation of the judicial and carceral systems that marked his final months of life: depositions, newspaper reports, prison entrance books, and the succinct punctuation of a death certificate. By combining the snippets with other sources, we can reconstruct the background of a young Aboriginal man living in the Hunter and Williams River valleys, and gain insight into his experience with Europeans and British law. We can scrutinise the events with white woman Jane Delanthy that led to Jim Crow's execution, and ask whether the evidence, by today's standards, would secure a conviction. This chapter illustrates how, despite Jim Crow's representation by one of the colony's most influential lawyers, William Charles Windeyer, the legal system placed him at a disadvantage. Ultimately, it appears unlikely that Jim Crow would have been executed had he been white rather than Aboriginal.

Alternate geography

The life that ended on a hangman's noose began, according to Jim Crow's death certificate, in Clarence Town, a small hamlet north east of Maitland situated on the southern part of the Williams River. He was born between 1835 and 1838, a time when the local Aboriginal groups were threatened by pastoral expansion and the establishment of new towns, with populations already drastically reduced through disease and frontier violence.[4] A relative lack of trees in the country surrounding the Williams River at the time of European arrival would have appealed to graziers and farmers, with English surgeon Peter Cunningham, who travelled north of the Hunter Valley in 1826, describing the banks of the Williams as "heavily timbered, but the forest land behind … open, grassy, and every way suitable for pasture without cutting down a single tree".[5] The first land grant near what became Clarence Town was made in 1823.[6] Others settlers soon followed, including the founders of a ship yard that became central to the town's fortunes in the colonial network of steamers.[7]

The name given to this locality by the Aboriginal people whom these new settlers were rapidly displacing is reportedly 'Erringhi' or 'Erring-I', said to mean 'Place of the Black Duck', although the origins of this name, including the language from which it derives, is unknown.[8] We can imagine the dismay of the Aboriginal inhabitants at this European encroachment, with the towns (in the words of Henry Reynolds) "suddenly appearing and then mush-rooming on their own traditional territory".[9]

The nature of clan boundaries in the area at the time of settlement is difficult to ascertain from the written record. Many ethnological works that sought to characterise language and grouping – such as Alfred Howitt's *Native Tribes of South-East Australia*, and John Fraser's *Aborigines of New South Wales* – were not published until the end of the nineteenth century, when the pre-contact way of life and tribal boundaries had been irreparably disrupted (although these sources often drew on earlier records).[10] Clarence Town is part of a wedge of land that Howitt claimed was inhabited by the Gringai group, which centred on the township of Dungog, 23 kilometres north of Clarence Town.[11] Gringai territory possibly extended as far east as Port Stephens, and as far west as the Paterson River,[12] and several contemporary texts today identify the Gringai people as a clan of either the Worimi to the east or the Wonnarua to the west.[13]

Rather than using terms such as Gringai and Worimi, the official colonial records from the 1830s and 1840s associated local Aborigines instead with nearby towns and stations. For example,

Justice of Peace George MacKenzie, when compiling a list of Aborigines who received blankets along the Williams River, made no record of Aboriginal names or affiliations, writing that "It is here almost if not wholly impossible to ascertain to what district any … family of the Aborigines Belong".[14] In their fixed European viewpoint, many settlers of this period did not properly understand the movements of Aboriginal groups across fixed boundaries. For example, in *Aborigines of the Hunter Valley*, Helen Brayshaw describes such rights of passage between neighbouring groups:

> This wide network of kinship ties and obligations extended economic and social links far beyond the core territory in which each horde habitually moved about collecting food, and it meant that others' territories could be visited, for example in pursuit of patchy resources, and when social, marital and other exchanges took place.[15]

Blanket lists, such as the one prepared by MacKenzie, are today rich fodder for historians. These were prepared by local distributors of government-issued blankets (often justices of the peace, police magistrates or police officers) and submitted to the Colonial Secretary. They included a name (usually both Aboriginal and English), estimated age, numbers of wives, number of children, and place of usual resort.[16] Less information was included on women, if they were listed individually at all,[17] and children usually only appeared as a number alongside the names of their fathers.[18] As demographic tools these lists are problematic. For example, the 1837 blanket returns from localities close to Clarence Town – Dungog, Newcastle, Gloucester and Port Stephens[19] – list more than 720 Aboriginal people, but an accompanying note to these documents states that only five of 12 expected returns from the North and North Western districts of the colony were submitted, indicating a huge data gap.[20] Furthermore, we can assume that not all Aboriginal people wished to be in contact with Europeans or receive blankets. Cultural affiliation is notoriously difficult to parse from these documents, as many Aboriginal people were displaced to distant localities, or formed new "mobs" with related groups as their population declined; each person may have differently experienced their overlapping connections to their old and new country.[21]

Clarence Town, the birthplace of Jim Crow, was never a blanket distribution point on its own, but appears briefly in the blanket returns for Dungog. The 1837 list includes a man named Marangat, said to be of the 'Clarence Town' tribe.[22] In 1838, Marangat again appears in the Dungog return, this time as part of the 'Boat Fall Tribe' of the Lower Williams, a possible reference to Boatfall Creek, a small stream about four kilometres east of Clarence Town.[23] ('Boatfall' also appears in the 1837 list, but its inhabitants at this time are eight women.[24]) In 1838, the list of men who are part of the Boatfall Tribe includes Marangat and eleven other men previously listed, in 1837, as being part of the Canninggalla Tribe, living at Canninggalla and the Upper Williams, north of Dungog.[25] The change in classification for these men most likely reflects the movements of Aboriginal populations within the region, a phenomenon that one imagines increased with the expansion of European settlement.[26] These movements also indicate that Aborigines living at Clarence Town were likely to be part of the same group as those living around Dungog: the Gringai. Jim Crow does not appear in these lists, as would be expected for a small child, but we can speculate that these Boatfall inhabitants may have been his people.

Two worlds meet

The years between Jim Crow's birth in Clarence Town and his arrest in 1860 are largely blank. The Dungog blanket return for 1842 (the next return after 1838) does not include entries for Clarence Town or Boat Fall. By contrast, we can gain an understanding of the European settlement's growth from the institutions and businesses established there during Jim Crow's early years: an official post office in 1839; the George and Dragon Inn in 1842; the local bench of magistrates in 1844.[27] In 1845, the submission of a Dr McKinlay of Dungog to the NSW Select Committee on the Condition of the Aborigines revealed that the native Gringai were struggling, largely from food shortages and disease.[28] Their number in the District of Dungog (which included Clarence Town) was estimated to be 63,[29] a figure starkly lower than the 152 in the Dungog list of 1838, which covered a similar region.[30] European settlement had within decades turned the local Aboriginal groups from thriving communities into fringe dwellers.[31]

Within the assimilationist project of colonial authorities in the early to mid nineteenth century, work was seen as a tool that not only inculcated discipline in Aborigines, but also created desires that would position them within the settler economy.[32] Aboriginal labour became particularly important from 1851, when the gold rushes lured European workers away from farms, and landholders found that the Aborigines could not only perform the much-needed work but often did so to a higher standard.[33] But this growing regard was bitter-sweet; even if Aboriginal workers were seen as a cut above the lowest white labourer, as Henry Reynolds argues, their race would always reduce them to the lowest strata of colonial society.[34] Jim Crow matured into adulthood as part of this economy, and at the time of the events that led to his trial, was employed as a labourer, travelling to various properties with "a machine", presumably an agricultural device.[35] Payment of Aborigines for work at this time varied widely, from rations alone to cash wages, and it is debatable what kind of income he would have earned.[36]

Standing at just five feet and one-and-a-half inches in height, Jim Crow was physically unimposing, but his intellectual ability may have been more impressive. Although his entrance record for Maitland Gaol is blank in the column headed 'Education',[37] a letter published in the *Maitland Mercury* several months after Jim Crow's execution suggests that he may received some sort of education. It was penned by Dungog resident David Marshall, who had attended a lecture by phrenologist AS Hamilton that featured a cast of Crow's head.

> I made up my mind to be present in consequence of having known the unfortunate aboriginal for a number of years; but what was my surprise when I heard Mr. Hamilton say that Jim Crow was an idiot! You may rely upon it, gentlemen, Mr. Hamilton is very much mistaken; for I can vouch for Jim Crow being one of the most intellectual blacks in the whole colony.[38]

David Marshall was possibly related to shipbuilder James Marshall, co-founder of Clarence Town's Deptford Shipyards, and as a local would therefore have been familiar with the remaining Aborigines on the town's fringes.[39] Did Marshall mean that Crow had received an education? That he perhaps was a deft conversationalist? Or did Jim Crow exhibit the bush nous settlers so often admired in Aboriginal people?

As mentioned in Chapter One, Colin Pardoe has suggested that Crow may have had a European parent.[40] If this were so, in the displacement wrought by colonialism, mixed parentage would have wedged him even deeper in the crack between two worlds.

"Give me rape, missus"

On 24 January 1860 at about 11am, Jim Crow visited a farmhouse in the township of Thalaba to ask for water. Situated near Dungog, the home belonged to William and Jane Delanthy. It was separated from the nearest neighbour by a quarter-of-a-mile of bush. Jane Delanthy, pregnant at the time, was home alone with her child, her husband being away at the threshing machine with other men from the area.[41] She did not have water to give the small Aboriginal man who wore a sleeve of his jumper on his head, but offered him coffee instead. While he sat on a stool and drank she made conversation, asking Jim Crow whom he worked for.

We can be fairly certain that Delanthy would have felt anxious during this encounter. Violence between settlers and Aborigines had led to a prevalent sense of insecurity in inter-racial contact, even when a flashpoint was not imminent.[42] In *Frontier*, Reynolds describes the psychological mark left on Queensland settlers by this conflict, and we can assume that this was similar in earlier frontiers: "the insecurity of the frontier had touched them all at one time or another. Fear had not been confined to those most exposed to attack; it often ran like fire, far from the point of conflagration".[43] Describing similar anxiety in Victoria, Bain Attwood has detailed the "terror and dread" felt by a clergyman's wife whenever Aborigines visited the family property.[44]

Shortly into Jim Crow's visit, the prosecution and defence stories diverge. According to Delanthy's evidence, Jim Crow now asked "Will you give me rape, Missus?" She reported that she had not understood him at first, and that he repeated this question twice more.

> I at length understood that he wanted to take liberties with me ... I told him to let me go out and get him what he wanted ... but he would not let me. I at length got out, but he kept near me, edging close to me and asking me to go inside, when I got to the end of the barn I ran and screamed, when I got a short distance beyond the barn, prisoner seized me and dragged me back opposite the barn, and threw me down, he then pulled down the fall of his trousers, pulled up my clothes, and jumped upon me.[45]

According to Jane Delanthy's testimony, Jim Crow twice penetrated her, despite her screams and continuous resistance. When she eventually struggled backwards from him and begged him not to hurt her, as she was "in the family way", Jim Crow told her he would not. They then both ran away, in different directions, she to the house of her neighbour Ann Hill.[46]

The depositions from the committal proceedings, taken by Justice of Peace John Hooke, include a brief statement from Jim Crow:

> I went to Delanthys [sic] house and asked for water, woman give me coffee, she then go out, I then go out and take the woman by the arm, knock her down, lift her clothes with me arm and pull it out of trousers with the other, I then hold him woman's leg, woman say I couldnt [sic] do it, and I then ran away, woman say don't hurt me.

The circumstances surrounding the making of this statement would end up being just a component of the procedural issues that disadvantaged Jim Crow in his trial, at which he pleaded not guilty. The conviction rate for sexual violence during the nineteenth century was much lower than for other violent crimes, but for Jim Crow the system was stacked against him.[47]

Procedural unfairness

Sixteen men were executed during the Maitland Gaol's 150-year history, the last in 1897. Of these, only three were executed for rape: Jim Crow; Irishman Michael Collihane in 1851, who had assailed a woman on the side of a country road while she waited for her husband with an injured cow; and in 1897 Charles Hines, who had sexually assaulted his step-daughter over several years.[48]

Historian of crime Amanda Kaladelfos argues that the greatest perceived threats to white womanhood in the bush were lower-class workers and Aborigines.[49] She writes that, throughout most of the nineteenth century, debates about whether the death penalty should be retained for rape (it had been abolished in Britain in 1841), focused on the perceived need for a penalty sufficiently grave as to deter these two groups. By viewing Jim Crow's case alongside others from the Maitland Circuit Court of 1860 and 1861, we can begin to see how the conviction was aided by Jane Delanthy's status as a 'virtuous' victim within the classic narrative of a vulnerable white woman in the bush.[50]

As in Jim Crow's case, the prosecutions of John Laver for attempted rape and Jeremiah Driscoll for rape both required the word of the alleged victim to be balanced against that of the defendant. But otherwise they could not have been more different.[51] These two cases originated in the working class area of Newcastle and, unlike in Jim Crow's case, where his social status was clearly inferior to that of Jane Delanthy, the women in Laver and Driscoll both knew their alleged attackers socially and were of the same class. Alcohol was involved in both instances: the husband of the victim in the Laver case, Elizabeth McPhee, drank with the accused the night before the alleged attempted rape; and the complainant, Annie Hicks, in Driscoll had personally been drinking with the defendant just before the crime was said to have occurred. Neither case succeeded. The jury in Laver's case could not come to an agreement and he was released with a bond of £100;[52] that no conviction resulted is probable since he was not readmitted to Maitland Gaol.[53] Meanwhile, the Driscoll trial was discontinued after evidence was presented that Annie Hicks's "character for chastity was not good".[54] These outcomes illustrate that for a prosecution to meet the high burden of proof, circumstantial factors such as class and virtue probably had to play a role.

Class and its impact on the validity of witness testimony also played a complex part in the third case, that of Billy and Tommy, two Aboriginal men charged with assaulting with intent Sarah Jane Spatch (between nine and ten years old) and Jessie Ellen

Spatch (between five and six) just one month before the events at Thalaba.[55] Sarah claimed to have been given a blood nose by Billy during the altercation in the bush with the two men, but Jessie had – according to her father's testimony – allegedly been hurt by Tommy "between the legs, in the privates". Both had scratched throats.[56] There was an issue of mistaken identity early in proceedings, with Sarah initially identifying another Aboriginal man named Jacky as her sister's aggressor, and the jury returned a verdict of not-guilty within just 15 minutes.[57] As children, the Spatches were not automatically considered reliable witnesses, and the validity of testimony depended on establishing that they understood the nature of an oath.[58] Only the older girl, Sarah Spatch, testified in the end, and she had to attest that she knew "I call God to witness that what I say is the truth".[59] Both Sarah and her father, William Spatch, were illiterate, signing their names with an X (as did Elizabeth McPhee), indicative of inferior social status.[60] Ultimately, mistaken identity played a major legal role in impugning the prosecution case, but in the contest of social status, the Spatches were also not as distant from their alleged aggressors as the literate Jane Delanthy was from Jim Crow.

There was also another crucial difference between Jim Crow's case and these three comparative cases: none of the other four defendants gave a statement during their committal proceedings, as was common for accused individuals with appropriate legal representation. The fact that Jim Crow did make a statement indicates that he may not have been represented at committal. The statement was ultimately not allowed at trial, after Jim Crow's lawyer, Windeyer, objected to its use, there being insufficient proof that he was twice warned that anything he might say would be used against him, as required by law.[61] But we can assume that the very fact one had been made may have alerted the jury to the possibility of prejudicial evidence.

Other issues with the statement include its not being signed, even with an X, as was the norm in such a legally crucial document, making it questionable whether Jim Crow felt it accurately reflected his side of events. Jim Crow did not have an interpreter at the committal proceeding, as was usual for Aboriginal defendants.[62] When this shortcoming was raised at trial, the judge pointed out that the statement was made in English, indicating his belief that no interpreter was required.[63] Yet, if we consider Delanthy's evidence, Jim Crow's level of English comprehension becomes questionable. The phrase "Give me rape" is an unusual construction, and not one that a fluent English speaker would make, as are phrases from Jim Crow's statement such as "I then hold him woman's leg".[64]

Furthermore, statements made during committal proceedings were recorded in such a way as to incorporate the questions of magistrates and justices of peace into the answers. It is therefore a distinct possibility that Jim Crow was simply answering 'yes' and 'no' to leading questions put to him, or repeating them in accented English, in the belief that compliance with the authorities would assist his case. That accused individuals often did not understand the impact of their statements is evident from a letter published after the trial in *The Maitland Mercury*, in which 'G' of Dungog argued that justices of the peace and clerks conducting committal proceedings should expand the warning to the accused that any statement made could be used against them. G suggested that they should include these words: "you have nothing to hope from any promise of favour".[65] More recently, the linguist Diane Eades has documented this phenomenon of concurrence by Aboriginal people within the twentieth century.[66] Eades says the tendency to agree is particularly strong when dealing with authority figures such as teachers or police officers. She typifies the psychology behind this major problem for Aboriginal people in the legal system thus: "'I think that if I say "yes" you will see that I am obliging, and socially amenable, and you will think well of me, and things will work out well between us.'"[67] But little would end well for Jim Crow.

Overall, the collection of statements and charges that make up the Jim Crow depositions are unusually thin for a capital case.

At just 13 pages, the depositions are the shortest of any from the first and second quarter of the 1860 Maitland Circuit Court. By contrast, the depositions for a case involving a robbed traveller are 23 pages long,[68] and the manslaughter case of a doctor charged with criminal negligence runs to 57 pages, reflecting how much more work was required to convict a person of higher status.[69]

The final issue related to procedural fairness was the jury's composition by white men. We can only guess at their potential antipathy towards Jim Crow if we consider Kristyn Harman's comments on an 1843 case before the Maitland Circuit Court in which seven Aboriginal men were tried. "The jurymen were drawn from amongst the landowners of the district, men that considered their persons and their property to be under threat from Aboriginal people."[70] Although this case occurred 17 years before Jim Crow's trial, virulent prejudice among white jurors continued to be noted as late as 1913 in the Northern Territory, when Judge Bevan and Chief Protector Stretton described most juries as "twelve men picked indiscriminately whose [view] is that the 'nigger' is something a good bit lower than a dog".[71]

The evidence reconsidered

Setting the unsigned statement aside, would there have been enough evidence by today's standards to convict Jim Crow of rape?

Jim Crow's court-appointed defence barrister, Windeyer, was a legal luminary of the Colony, a member of the NSW Legislative Assembly, scion of a family of powerful Hunter Valley landholders, and future Supreme Court Judge who would preside over such infamous cases as the Mt Rennie rape trial.[72] He had also successfully defended Laver and Billy and Tommy in their respective trials. Yet his key arguments in Jim Crow's trial were summarised by the *Maitland Mercury* in so perfunctory a fashion as to suggest an editorial bias in reporting cases with Aboriginal parties:

> Mr Windeyer ... [contended] that the circumstances as
> related by the principal witness were of such an improbable
> character as to throw suspicion upon the case, and to lead to
> the conclusion that, though she might have been frightened ...
> he had not committed the crime with which he was charged,
> but she had been induced to make that charge by fear or some
> other motive, in the first instance, and subsequently to adhere
> to it for the sake of her own character. He also urged some
> other arguments in the prisoner's favour.[73]

Windeyer homed in on the time it took Delanthy to report the
rape to her husband and police. William Delanthy returned home
at about 8 pm on the day of the attack, and although Jane told
him she had been "ill-used by a black" that night she did not
"tell all" until the next day, when her husband asked for further
details.[74] One might argue that a traumatising experience such as
rape would have affected Delanthy so profoundly that her husband
could only have asked her to "tell all" that very night. Ann Hill
similarly deposed that Delanthy had said she had been "badly
used by a black", rather than mentioning rape, to account for her
"wild appearance" and torn dress, and had told Hill "Oh I am
nearly killed by a black".[75] But there was no evidence submitted
of physical harm to suggest attempted murder, and the fact that
Crow ran away from the scene implies Delanthy was not at risk of
being killed. In querying whether Crow committed the crime, we
might also consider his small stature; could he have overpowered
Delanthy? Without knowing her height and build this is of course
difficult to judge.

On the evidence, there are several possibilities for what happened
after Crow drank his coffee. The first is that, rather than saying
"give me rape", he had asked for something completely different.
This is likely when we consider the oddness of a rapist asking
his victim to allow herself to be raped, considering that the very
essence of rape is force. He may instead have been asking for food.

The Dungog police constable, James Bannister, when examined during the trial, said that Crow had told him (during questioning), that "he then asked her for something to eat, and with that, she ran out of the house, and he followed her and caught her by the arm, and she lay down".[76] It is not clear what Jim Crow means by Delanthy "lying" down. The interpretation most sympathetic to Jim Crow would be that, after she misunderstood his request for food, he followed her from the house out of bewilderment or concern, attempted to placate her, and that she then fell over in hysteria. Confused and potentially aware of the ramifications of displeasing a white person, Jim Crow ran away into the bush. The next day, upset that her husband was dismissive of the 'attack', perhaps Jane Delanthy alleged rape in order to be taken seriously. Or perhaps William Delanthy himself encouraged his wife to fabricate a claim out of racial prejudice.

The phrase "lying down" offers other possibilities. One is that Jane Delanthy consented to sex with Jim Crow, although this is unlikely when we consider the disparity in social status and her "wild state" of distress. The other is that he did drag her to the ground with the intention of raping her, but decided to stop before actually doing so. This interpretation would correlate with Jim Crow's problematic committal statement, in which he does not actually admit to penetrating Delanthy.

Finally, it is of course possible that Jim Crow did rape Delanthy as claimed. The contemporary understanding of the trauma caused by rape is that it will result in some victims never reporting the crime at all, or not doing so for many years. In that sense, Delanthy's failure to elaborate until the following morning that "ill use" in fact amounted to rape is unremarkable, especially if we consider the aspersions cast on alleged rape victims at the time, as exemplified by the Driscoll case. Did Delanthy perhaps fear that her husband would accuse her of provoking the attack? If Jim Crow did rape Delanthy, the motive was probably far more complex than just sexual desire. In describing a Victorian case involving the rape of a white woman, Bain Attwood argues that the rape represented "a desperate assertion of power by an Aboriginal man who was himself oppressed by a particular racial and gender structure".[77] A similar motive of acting against the power imbalance is hinted at in something Jane Delanthy said to Jim Crow during the committal proceeding: "You asked me whose ground it was[.] I said it was mine."[78] For a man such as Crow displaced from his country, rape may have become a retaliatory reflex.

Ultimately, we will never know what happened at Thalaba, but the evidence does not appear strong enough to have secured a guilty verdict in a case of contesting stories. We can speculate that the jury may itself have been divided. According to the *Maitland Mercury*'s account of the trial, after deliberating Jim Crow's guilt for half an hour, it asked a question of Justice John Nodes Dickinson. Shortly after this unspecified question was answered, the jurors found Jim Crow guilty but recommended him to mercy.[79] Could the jury have made this recommendation because it did not feel altogether satisfied by the prosecution's side of events and so was reluctant to send this man to the gallows? Was this a matter of male solidarity?

But the matter of penalty was for Judge Dickinson to determine. Kaladelfos notes that, between 1841 and 1901, one in three Aboriginal men convicted of rape were executed, compared to one in seven European men.[80] Aboriginal offenders were also less likely to have their sentences commuted.[81] Dickinson had shown mercy in 1848 in the case of another Aboriginal man, Darby, convicted of raping a European woman, and passed a sentence of 'death recorded'.[82] According to the *Maitland Mercury*, Dickinson "did not think [Darby]'s education and opportunities could have fitted him for an early death, and because he thought the example of such a being losing his life was more likely to excite commiseration and pity than to act as a warning".[83] This statement combined speculation on the deterrent role of execution with prevailing humanitarian ideas of the mid-nineteenth century. But the intervening 12 years to 1860, and the wearing monotony of other rape trials, had presumably leeched away at Dickinson's compassion.

In the close-knit networks of colonial New South Wales, relations between Windeyer and the judiciary were also strained around this time. The preceding year, in his capacity as member of the Legislative Assembly, Windeyer had vociferously opposed Chief Justice Alfred Stephen's application to take extended leave at full pay, an application ultimately approved.[84] Just a few months into Stephen's absence, Windeyer came before his bench-mate Dickinson in the cases of Billy and Tommy and Jim Crow, and we can wonder how this impacted on the penalty that the judge thought most appropriate for the convicted rapist. Dickinson did not follow the jury's recommendation of mercy. He promptly sentenced Jim Crow to death.

Conclusion: "In a few moments, the souls were in eternity"

Jim Crow was born and raised at a time when his people and country were being squeezed into a foreign form of sovereignty that would only ever allow them a marginal role. His committal, trial and death sentence reflect a pattern of discriminatory attitudes towards Aboriginal men in the criminal justice system. Regardless of the disempowered position of women in colonial society, Aboriginal men ranked significantly lower, a disparity that potentially helped to secure Jim Crow's conviction.

After being terminated so abruptly on a scaffold, his brief lifetime was about to be overshadowed by a bizarre series of events. Just minutes after Jim Crow was executed, the phrenologist AS Hamilton took a plaster cast of his head, and would return later for the real thing. After months of confinement in the Maitland Gaol, and internment in the ground, Jim Crow would travel.

The Scottish phrenologist AS Hamilton
holding a miniature bust of Prince Albert.
(Hobart Archives and Heritage Office, SC89/1/2 1871 48,
Documents in Cases of Divorce – Hamilton v Hamilton)

Agnes Hamilton, third wife of the phrenologist AS Hamilton,
sat for her portrait during a stay in Stawell, Victoria.
(Agnes Hamilton-Grey photographs, PXA1231,
Mitchell Library, State Library of New South Wales)

PHRENOLOGY, the science of mind, is the most complete system of mental philosophy.

The brain is the organ of the mind, the physical instrument of thought and feeling.

The mind consists of a plurality of independent faculties, each of which exercises a distinct class of functions.

The brain consists of as many different portions, called organs, as the mind does of faculties.

Other conditions being equal, the size of the brain and of each organ is the measure of their power.

The peculiar character of man is ascertained by the comparative size of his phrenological organs.

An Estimate of the Character of *Master Walter Filmer*

Date _____ 18

Age _____ years,

BY

MR. A. S. HAMILTON,
PRACTICAL PHRENOLOGIST.

The study of Phrenology constitutes an important duty of the human race. All the power of this Divine work of wonderful Machinery—the Human Mind—with sensation, judgment, memory, and volition, impart to man his distinctive character, and highly exalt him in relation to the other created beings by which he is surrounded. The Human Mind is man's noble distinction in every state of life. It is the source of his happiness or his misery. It is the beginning of all the superior actions connected with his existence. It is that which we train and develop from the ignorance and weakness of infancy, into the knowledge, the wisdom, and the strength of manhood. Great evils to mankind have resulted from the unrestrained action of the mental faculties, especially when their liability to err has been fostered and encouraged by a false system of education, and by flattery. "It is of vital importance, therefore, that the innate dispositions be well understood by parents and teachers, in order to enable them to quicken in youth, by exercise, those powers which are productive of knowledge and virtue, and keeping in due bounds those which, in their abuse, are productive of evil.

"Europe, the centre and focus of all the lights in the world, has its philosophy only in expectation."—DUGALD STEWART.

"Phrenology presents the first practical mental philosophy known of man."—R. AND W. CHAMBERS.

"Look at Phrenology in France, in Britain, and in the United States of America. It already directs Lunatic Asylums, it presides over Education, it mitigates the severity of the Criminal Law, it assuages religious animosity, it guides the Historian, it is a beacon light to the Physiologist, and already has incorporated its nomenclature with the Languages of these Countries."—G. COMBE.

Measurement with Tape Line.

	INCHES.		INCHES.
Circumference of the head		From the opening of the ear to Individuality	
Length from occipital spine to Individuality		Constructiveness to ditto, over Benevolence	
From ear to ear, over Firmness		Self-esteem to Comparison	
From Cautiousness to ditto			

Temperaments or Quality of Brain.

The BILIOUS Temperament is recognised by black, hard, and wiry hair, dark or black eyes, dark skin, moderate fulness, but much firmness of flesh, with a harsh outline of countenance and person. This is the temperament for mental as well as bodily labour.

The NERVOUS Temperament is indicated by silky thin hair, thin skin, small thin muscles, quick muscular motion, paleness, and often delicate health. It is the marked temperament for genius and refinement.

The SANGUINE Temperament is distinguished by light or red hair, blue eyes, fair and often ruddy countenance, well defined person, plumpness, and firmness of muscle, great activity of the blood-vessel, and a fondness for active exertion.

The LYMPHATIC is indicated by roundness of person, pale skin, fair hair, soft flesh, softness of muscle, and full cellular tissue. The vital action is languid, the circulation weak and slow, the brain feeble in its action, and the mental manifestations proportionately sluggish.

Relative Proportion of the Organs.

VERY LARGE 20, LARGE 18, NEARLY LARGE 16, VERY FULL 14, FULL 12, MODERATE 10, SMALL 8.

Note.—The Organs marked "Very Large," "Large," and "Rather Large," are those that are naturally most powerful, and which may be most easily cultivated, and in some instances need to be restrained. Those marked "Very Full," "Full," and "Moderate," are Organs capable of being quickened and improved by exercise. And those marked "Small," are those that are most feeble, and which will be most difficult to excite to powerful activity.

ORGANS AND THEIR FUNCTIONS.
ORDER 1—FEELINGS.—GENUS 1—PROPENSITIES.

18 1. *Amativeness.*—Sexual Love.

19 2. *Philoprogenitiveness.*—Love of offspring.

16 3. *Inhabitiveness.*—Attachment to place.

16 3a. *Concentrativeness.*—The power of concentrating feeling and ideas, ploddingness, concentrated application.

18 4. *Adhesiveness.*—Attachment to persons and objects, animate and inanimate, social sympathy, friendship.

17 5. *Combativeness.*—Physical courage, opposiveness.

19 6. *Destructiveness.*—Executiveness, overcoming power.

17 6a. *Love of Life.*—Instinctive tendency to cling to life.

18 6b. *Alimentiveness.*—Prompts to take nourishment and make choice of food.

17¼ 7. *Secretiveness.*—Power to conceal the thoughts, motives, and desires.

(Above and right) Phrenological Report of Walter Filmer by AS Hamilton.

(Courtesy of Newcastle Museum)

9. *Acquisitiveness.*—The desire to acquire in general the sense of property, industry.

Constructiveness.—A tendency to construct in general, but is directed by the other faculties.

GENUS II.—Sentiments.   1.—*Sentiments common to Man and the Lower Animals.*

10. *Self-esteem.*—Self-reliance, dignity, individuality of character.

11. *Love of Approbation.*—Produces the desire of the esteem and approbation of others, courtesy.

12. *Cautiousness.*—Produces the emotion of fear in acting and speaking, circumspection, prudence.

2.—*Sentiments proper to Man.*

13. *Benevolence.*—Disinterestedness, compassion, charity.

14. *Veneration.*—Reverence, deference, devotion, self-abasement.

15. *Firmness.*—Endurance, determination, constancy, and perseverance.

16. *Conscientiousness.*—Imparts the sense of justice, respects the rights of others, consistency.

17. *Hope.*—Anticipates the fulfilment of what the other faculties desire.

18. *Wonder–Faith.*—Credulity—Imagination—produces the disposition to delight in what is new and extraordinary.

19. *Ideality.*—Produces the sentiment of beauty and perfectibility.

19a. *Sublimity.*—Enjoys and takes cognizance of the sublime.

20. *Imitation.*—Gives the disposition to imitate in general.

INTELLECTUAL FACULTIES.

GENUS I.—Perceptives.

21. *Individuality.*—Imparts the power of observing and remembering specific individual existences, and their names.

22. *Form.*—Imparts the talent of observing and remembering the configuration of bodies.

23. *Size.*—Enables us to observe and remember the dimensions of bodies.

24. *Weight.*—Gives the talent of observing, appreciating, and remembering the resistance and momentum of bodies.

25. *Colour.*—Communicates the talent of perceiving and remembering colours—capacity for painting.

26. *Locality.*—Imparts the power of observing and remembering the relative positions of bodies and places, gives talent for grouping, geography, navigation, &c., &c.

27. *Number.*—Confers the talent for calculation, arithmetical ability.

28. *Order.*—Communicates the talent of observing and remembering the arrangements of objects, and confers an aptitude for methodical arrangements.

29. *Eventuality.*—Imparts the power of observing and remembering events and occurrences of every kind, and conduces to the talent for practical details in the affairs of life.

30. *Time.*—Enables us to perceive and remember duration, or the relation which one thing bears to another in time.

31. *Tune.*—Imparts the power of perceiving and remembering melody, talent for melody.

32. *Language.*—The power of perceiving and remembering the signs of our ideas, likewise of acquiring languages, and expressing ideas in words.

GENUS II.—Reflectives.

33. *Comparison.*—Gives the power of discovering resemblances, analogies, either among things or ideas, and disposes to the use of figurative language.

34. *Causality.*—Traces the relation between cause and effect, and the dependencies of phenomena, metaphysical and logical talent.

35. *(Wit.)*—To perceive differences in ideas, inconsistencies, incongruities, and contrasts—to expose and enjoy the ludicrous.

Temperament.

(Supposing it to be represented by the term 8.)

Nervous *2*;   Sanguine *2½*;   Bilious *2*;   Lymphatic *1½*.

TERMS:

Verbal description of Character, with Chart and Scale of Organs, 5s.   Written description, with scale of Organs and Advice for Self-improvement and the proper application of the Mental Powers, 10s.   Complete Study, £1.

A remarkably active and energetic and vigorous head — Full of

The *SS Konoowarra*, the ship on which the Hamilton collection
was transported to Melbourne. Lithograph by J Sands, 1883.

(State Library of Victoria)

PHRENOLOGY REFUTED.

BETTER HALF.— *What is the matter, my Love?*
WORSE HALF.— *Why, that fool of a Phrenological Professor says I
have obstinacy and self-esteem large. I've a great mind to break his head
for it. Nothing earthly shall convince me that, if there's any truth in
Phrenology, it oughtn't to be firmness and benevolence.*

Phrenology was front and centre in the public consciousness,
as demonstrated by this cartoon published in
Melbourne Punch, Vol. 1, p. 108, 1855.

(Rare Books Collection, State Library of Victoria)

Chapter Three

Scottish Head Case

20 July 1860

It was seven o'clock and darkness had long settled on Maitland by the time William House made his way to the inn of Mr Finch to respond to a request that he call upon one of the guests.[1]

Upon his arrival, the man who had summoned him quickly materialised, a figure familiar not only to House, sexton of St Peter's Church of England cemetery in East Maitland, but also to other townspeople.[2] The phrenologist Archibald Sillars Hamilton, known professionally as 'AS', had been lecturing throughout the region for some four months, using skulls and casts of heads to illustrate his craft of reading moral and intellectual characters from anatomy.[3]

Now, he took House out to the inn's verandah, and asked him if he recalled the double execution of Jim Crow and John Jones, and could he say whereabouts in the graveyard the two men might be buried.[4]

Mr House told him they were in the corner closest to the gate. And in which direction did the heads lie? House replied that they lay to the west, in the manner of all Christian burials.[5] In fact, Hamilton well knew where the graves were located. He had already visited the cemetery, and had confirmed the location of the graves with two people – an unknown young man, and the water carrier who had transported the bodies from gaol to cemetery.[6]

Now, Hamilton told House that he had observed the soil of the graves to be moist and easy to work with. He would pay the man one pound if he dug down to the coffins, unscrewed the lids and removed the heads of the two executed men. It was a simple task for a moonlit night.[7] House recoiled. The law would not apply to these men, Hamilton counselled; they were executed prisoners, and the police magistrate, Edward Denny Day, would have let him take the heads on execution day had there not been so many people about in the gaolyard.[8] The sexton said he would not do it and, even if he were permitted by church authorities, his health prevented it and he would need to hire an assistant. Nevertheless, he promised to call on Monday to provide his answer.[9]

Over the next few days, House began to wrestle with growing unease.[10] On Sunday, he recounted the conversation to the Reverend John Albert Greaves, parson of St Peter's. The next day Greaves visited the police magistrate, Day, to report the matter, only to find that the church warden Edward Ogg had already beaten him to it.[11] Day, who later denied ever telling Hamilton that he could have the heads, issued a summons for the phrenologist's arrest.[12]

Hamilton may have etched a profile for himself in the district, but moonlit nights and posthumous beheadings were apparently beyond the pale. He was bailed and committed to stand trial. The alleged crime: inciting another to exhume corpses from a burial ground.[13]

Science with a shovel

Hamilton's request on a winter's night in pastoral New South Wales was hardly unique. During the nineteenth century, enthusiasts of comparative anatomy and practices such as phrenology were scouring Australia for the skeletal remains of Aboriginal people, often aided by a network of paid collectors. Other parties to this scramble included curio hunters, museum directors and amateur enthusiasts.[14] This macabre fascination with collecting human remains resulted from a perfect storm of expanding empire, debates about human origin, and the rise of the discipline of anatomy.

Bronwen Douglas and Chris Ballard, historians of the body and colonialism, point to the era of oceanic exploration after 1750 as contributing to the development of a new idea of race in European scientific thought.[15] This period, best characterised in the Australian context through the voyages of Captain James Cook, brought European naturalists into contact with an increasing range of exotic humans. In a time when savants of the British Royal Society and French Academy of Sciences were developing taxonomies for plants and animals, this human diversity seemed to call for its own system of organisation through the lens of comparative anatomy.[16]

These new ideas for categorising human 'types' signalled a divergence from the humanistic views of Enlightenment thinkers, who attributed the presence and absence of 'civilisation' in different cultures to environment and opportunity.[17] In the Enlightenment conception, all humans, regardless of how far they progressed, had equal intellectual and moral potential. From the late 1700s, however, the view of a single origin, known as monogeny, was challenged by polygenists, who argued that different races were the product of divergent species.[18] The boundaries were immutable, and white Europeans were necessarily at the apex.

From the fray between monogenists and polygenists the new discipline of anthropology emerged in the 1830s, embracing polygenism in its study of humans.[19] Polygenist intellectuals penned racially and politically influential texts such as *The Negro's Place in Nature* (by James Hunt), and the argument of multiple origins became popular in pro-slavery circles.[20] In arguing their cases, both sides sought skeletal remains from around the world, with the remains of Aboriginal Australians a particular prize.[21]

The arrival in 1859 of Charles Darwin's *On the Origin of Species* established a common origin for humankind,[22] but the Darwinian position of shared ancestry did not signal a return to softer racial distinctions. Instead, Darwin's 1871 book *The Descent of Man* explained that 'primitive' races such as Tasmanian Aborigines were distant forebears, incapable of living like the 'civilised' Europeans whose world and intellect had evolved through millennia of development.[23] A racial hierarchy thus remained dominant in what historians today call Social Darwinism (Darwin's cousin Francis Galton, the father of eugenics, was highly impressed by *Origin of Species*).[24] The nineteenth century also saw a formalisation of dissection within medical education, and broader debates took place in Britain about the supply of dead bodies to medical schools for training, culminating in the *Anatomy Act* of 1832.[25]

But it would be incorrect to assume that this medical and scientific context rendered exhumation of Aboriginal graves universally acceptable. Paul Turnbull has documented examples from the first 50 years after 1788 that demonstrate the respect of many European settlers and colonial officials for Aboriginal graves and remains.[26] In Hamilton's case, the response by Reverend Greaves of reporting the phrenologist to the police indicates a belief that Jim Crow was as deserving of respectful burial as the European Jones.

Phrenology: all in the head

Hamilton's income and growing notoriety derived from a discipline that placed more emphasis on the head than ever before. At the end of the eighteenth century in Vienna, a physician named Franz Joseph Gall developed a new theory on the relationship between intellect, morality and the brain, and by extension its casing.[27] He identified twenty-seven sections of the brain – known as separate 'organs' – that controlled faculties as diverse as parental love, powers of concentration, attachment and social sympathy, secretiveness and friendship.[28] These corresponded with external regions of the skull. The number of organs would grow and their meanings would be adapted as its greatest proponents disseminated the discipline across Europe and out to the colonies, but in all its iterations, phrenology still retained the fundamental idea of the skull's shape providing clues to the brain within.[29]

Gall took his system abroad in the early years of the nineteenth century, accompanied by his assistant Johann Gaspar Spurzheim, but it was the latter's showmanship from 1814 on a lecture tour of Great Britain that catapulted the discipline into a position where, by the late 1830s, there were 29 phrenological societies in Britain alone.[30] Historian of science John van Wyhe writes that by the 1840s "phrenology was known to practically every person" in Britain, with thousands of phrenologists plying their trade.[31] The great driver behind this popularity was a Scotsman named George Combe, who moulded phrenology into a system for self-improvement, and whose 1828 *Constitution of Man* has been described by historian Roger Cooter as "one of the most esteemed and popular books of the second third of the nineteenth century", selling 300,000 copies by 1860.[32] Cooter argues that phrenology's great popular success derived from its allowing anybody to penetrate the depths of human character simply by running their fingers over a head, quite literally putting science in the hands of the populace.[33]

While today we easily pin the term 'pseudoscience' onto this practice, we should remember that phrenology was the subject of serious academic debate among doctors, anatomists and naturalists for much of the nineteenth century. Its adherents included Alfred Russel Wallace, considered a co-founder of the theory of evolution, who stood by his belief in phrenology until his death in 1913.[34] Furthermore, the term 'pseudoscience' implies that the boundaries of 'science' themselves are watertight, rather than resulting from negotiations and debates within and around the academy. For many people of this period, phrenology *was* science, and Cooter points out that advances in neurophysiology in the later nineteenth-century lent new credence to phrenology by proving relationships between brain and behaviour.[35]

Phrenology, and how it could best be applied, meant different things to different people, and it was by turns applied to a range of reform causes including universal suffrage, temperance, health and slavery abolition.[36] That it could serve contradictory purposes is evident from the fact that it was on one hand viciously attacked as a materialist system that denied the role of God in human thought or behaviour but, on the other, was also adopted by scientifically minded clergyman, a group whom David de Giustino terms 'Christian Phrenologists'.[37] An Australian example of this latter group was the Reverend B Bottomley, phrenologist and physiognomist, who delivered lectures and gave readings in Queensland during the 1890s.[38] Phrenology's use as a tool for self-improvement also correlated with a nineteenth-century preoccupation with keeping working classes appropriately occupied so as to reduce time available for social disturbance,[39] a principle that explains its prominent role within mechanics' institutes.[40] In the spirit of social experimentation, phrenology would also play a role in the administration of prisons and mental asylums.[41]

Antipodean story

In 1896, one of the canonical Australian writers of prose and verse, Henry Lawson, published a major collection of short fiction that included the melancholy 'Story of Malachi'.[42] In this sometimes heart-wrenching, sometimes sentimental tale set on a cattle station, the unnamed narrator describes the practical jokes that he and his fellow workers played on the simpleton labourer Malachi. For their greatest joke, the men convinced Malachi that a visiting bricklayer who knew some phrenology "was suspected of having killed several persons for experimental purposes". On the last night that "Bricky" stayed at the station, he entered Malachi's hut, carrying a bag with a pumpkin at the bottom of it. To the amusement of the men observing through a crack in the bark, Bricky began to make overtures towards Malachi's skull.

"I've got Jimmy Nowlett's skull here," and he lifted the bag and lovingly felt the pumpkin... "I spoilt one of his best bumps with the tomahawk. I had to hit him twice, but it's no use crying over spilt milk." Here he drew a heavy shingling-hammer out of the bag and wiped off with his sleeve something that looked like blood. Malachi had been edging round for the door, and now he made a rush for it. But the skull-fancier was there before him.[43]

As a popular work of literature from the late nineteenth century, 'The Story of Malachi' demonstrates just how familiar the tropes of bump reading and skull thieving had become in Australia's colonies. The public understanding of phrenology can also be inferred from a short story by the lesser-known author 'Tasma' (Jessie Couvreur) published in 1878, in which she describes her female character as "romantic – for romantic, read largely endowed with the organ of Ideality".[44] Published in a collection of short stories for Christmas, the story never mentions the term 'phrenology', assuming literacy of the system among its readers, and particularly what the "organ of Ideality" would signify.

Phrenology arrived in Australia as early as the 1820s, claims Jan Evelyn Wilson, whose 1994 PhD thesis charted the practice's position alongside other nineteenth-century concerns – religion, penal reform, treatment of lunatics.[45] Wilson's is the most conclusive study of phrenology across the century, but phrenology has also been examined by various historians interested in its ties to race or crime.[46] In 1993, John Thearle tried to chart the clear point of decline for phrenology in Australia, but we should be wary of attempts to map an even rise and fall of such a popular practice.[47] As demonstrated by the resurgence of scientific interest in phrenology during the late nineteenth century, fantastically popular practices are protean – they will be applied in a variety of ways and will come in and out of fashion. In recent years, reproductions of the iconic phrenological head produced by the enterprising Fowler family of the US have come to populate gift shops, decorative pieces that exemplify the tongue-in-cheek antiquarian aesthetic currently in vogue. Online poster dealers sell large-scale phrenological charts. Do purchasers appreciate these artefacts just for their beauty, their artful representation of the human form, or do they perhaps also see in them a connection between mind and body that resonates with contemporary alternative health philosophies?

The newspaper digitisation project of the National Library of Australia, Trove, is now unveiling the true penetration of phrenology in the mid-to-late nineteenth and early twentieth centuries, with Hamilton just one among a constellation of showmen and women winking at the historian from advertisements and articles. The entertainment goal of many popular phrenologists is evident from an 1877 advertisement for a lecture by phrenologist Dr Carr, whose show included "laughable and marvellous experiments in electro-biology, hypnotism, mesmeric, somnambulism and electrical psychology", all accompanied by "appropriate music".[48] A performance by phrenologist Madame Sibly in South Australia in 1880 also included "a mesmeric extravaganza".[49] A sobering reminder of phrenology's cooption as a race science resonates in an 1890 advertisement for a lecture by "Professor J.A. Fritz, phrenologist and anatomist, who brought with him "a family of Bosjesmans, the smallest human race in the world, natives of Central Africa".[50]

In this dubious collective, few phrenologists command as many column inches as Archibald Sillars Hamilton. Born in or before 1819 in Ayrshire, Scotland, just a few years after Spurzheim embarked on his defining lecture tour of Britain, AS Hamilton grew up as phrenology reached a frenzy of popularity.[51] His father, Edward Hamilton, was a muslin manufacturer, but it was the influence of his mother, the popular phrenologist Agnes Sillars Hamilton, that would determine his future livelihood.[52] He described her to his third wife as "the first lady lecturess in Scotland, & of Great Britain", a woman whose maiden lecture, on the topic of bishops in the House of Lords, ended in her being "carried, instead of driven to her home, enthusiastically".[53] Cooter writes that Mrs Hamilton was "highly successful at drawing large audiences", and that she was a fierce advocate for the mental equality of men and women, although those phrenologists seeking respectability regarded her "as a quack", and one client termed her a "dirty old wench".[54] An 1859 advertisement in *The Falkirk Herald* for one of Mrs Hamilton's lectures also promised that "John S Hamilton, aged 8 years, will illustrate the Subject by singing in various styles". The enlistment of this child, presumably a grandson of Mrs Hamilton and nephew of Archibald Sillars Hamilton, demonstrates how the Scottish phrenologist might himself have been steeped in both phrenology and showmanship (or show*wo*manship) from an early age.[55]

With such strong beginnings, it is little wonder that by 1841 – when AS Hamilton was just in his early twenties and providing evidence in the committal proceedings of a newspaper publisher charged with embezzlement – he gave his profession as "phrenologist".[56] Hamilton arrived in Australia in November 1854, transplanted to the colonies just as phrenology had been.[57] Over the next 30 years, he would lecture and give private readings across Tasmania, Victoria, New South Wales, Queensland and both of New Zealand's islands in capital cities and regional centres.

A private customer of Hamilton's in 1854 could opt for either a description of their character with advice (3 shillings, 6 pence), a written sketch of character (5 shillings), or a detailed character reading with a phrenological chart (10 shillings).[58] Meanwhile, the more expensive phrenological chart gave a numerical value for each of the 'organs' of character and intellect in the brain. Parents would often take their children to see Hamilton for advice on future careers, his summations of character seemingly general enough to apply to most children. For example, in an 1855 character sketch of Quaker boy Robert Walker he wrote: "He is fond of animals and passionately delighted with play ... He requires a great deal of advice and guidance as he is so very impulsive".[59]

Perhaps the most significant of Hamilton's phrenological readings was carried out on the head of Mr Wilson Esquire in January
1880. Hamilton advised this 23-year-old man:

> You are best fitted for a profession in which quick observ-
> ation, penetrating intelligence lively wit, good language
> and logical acumen are indispensible. You have more than
> ordinary courage and excellent self-possession ... You
> require a little more patience, reserve, acquisitiveness, tact,
> diplomacy and management in the strict financial and
> prudential sense.

Hamilton thought that Mr Wilson would make a good advocate, or
that, with "a few years study" of political economy, social science,
natural theology, phrenology, psychology and human physiology,
he could "make [his] way successfully as a member of parliament".

The assessment was correct in substance, but underestimated
the potential of this singular young man. Hamilton was not pal-
pating the skull of Mr Wilson Esquire. This tall, dark-haired
person who had assumed the name of Wilson was in fact Alfred
Deakin, lawyer, journalist, spiritualist, and future Prime Minister
of Australia.[60] Deakin had already been elected to the Victorian
parliamentary seat of West Bourke the previous year, but resigned
in his maiden speech following claims about unfair polling. When
he sat for Hamilton, his ideas and ambitions may have been in a
state of turmoil, prompting him to seek vocational guidance under
an assumed name to assure an unbiased assessment. Just weeks
after the phrenological reading, he would lose the election for his
seat, only to regain it by July 1880.[61]

We can wonder whether the phrenologist would have made
similar conclusions about the younger man's proficiencies were he
wise to the deception:

> Though you have a good head, an active constitution & a mind
> of much general cleverness, & great clearness & capacity for
> using your intellect adavantageously, you are not an original
> nor profound thinker & have not great force of character.
> Yours is an intellect of ability, not genious [sic].

Or perhaps Hamilton had gauged the true identity of his sitter, or
been tipped off, and believed that some further education would
temper the impulsiveness of Deakin's youth and provide a better
grounding for what was at this stage a wavering political career.

The phrenologist after all took a keen interest in civic and political life, donating lecture proceeds to charity, running for public
office, and campaigning against capital punishment. In his role as
provocateur, he held enough public influence to chair a meeting in
1880 of more than 4000 Melburnians campaigning for Ned Kelly's
conviction to be overturned, and visited the Governor with Kate
Kelly on the day of the execution to plead for a reprieve.[62]

The only surviving photograph of Hamilton (to our knowledge)
is a *carte de visite* taken by Archibald McDonald, whose studio was
based in Melbourne's St George's Hall, Bourke Street East, between
roughly 1864 and 1873.[63] The extant newspaper advertisements and
articles that reveal Hamilton's movements suggest that he did not
return to Victoria until the late 1860s after a stint in New Zealand,
meaning that by the time he posed for McDonald he was in his late
forties.[64] Hamilton's wavy hair had receded so far by this stage as
to truly accentuate what his third wife referred to as his "colossal
forehead".[65] His eyes sternly meet the viewer, and in a reference
to his livelihood he grasps a miniature bust of Prince Albert (who
is said to have "appreciated deeply the phrenological advice that
he sought from time to time"), pointing with his other hand to
the prince consort's forehead.[66] Perhaps it is the combination of
the droopiness created by the full beard and moustache, the severe
nature of Victorian-era posture, and the heavy lines that connect

Hamilton's nose and mouth, but the expression in the phrenologist's wide eyes is melancholy.

Hamilton was a beneficiary of a career that focused on the human head, and it is perhaps fitting that it was into the cavity behind this colossal forehead that the grim reaper would strike him. In 1884, after 30 years lecturing in Australia, he died in Redfern from 'Effusion on the Brain'.[67]

Difference and deviance

Hamilton's urge to collect Jim Crow's skull can be seen as emblematic of phrenology's obsession with race. Paul Turnbull describes how Gall, phrenology's founder, argued "that the typical shape of various African crania reflected the relative size of the various discrete parts of the brain which he believed gave rise to specific qualities of intellect and emotion".[68] For his part, George Combe, the founder of the Edinburgh Phrenological Society, wrote in his phenomenally popular *Constitution of Man* that Aborigines were "distinguished by great deficiencies in the moral and intellectual organs".[69] Likewise, in 1868, Melbourne-based phrenologist Philemon Sohier submitted a report to the Select Committee of the Legislative Council of Victoria on Aborigines, in which he used terms such as "small, feeble and inactive", "deceitful, suspicious and slippery", "below mediocrity" and incapable of being "permanently improved".[70]

Hamilton's lectures featured the skulls of individuals who he said exemplified moral weakness and deviancy, with a primary focus on criminals and Aborginal people. His views on the capacity of Aborigines are evidenced by the labels attached to several of the skulls in the collection:

> No. 8. New Zealand Aboriginal. Maori Chief. Marks of Tattoo. Powerful brain – Striking contrast to Tasmanian.[71]

No. 10. Tasmanian Aboriginal Female. Lowest type of barbarian life. Weakness, timidity & Semi-imbecility.[72]

No. 55. Tasmanian Male. W[ea]kness Timidity... Contrasts with New Zealander.[73]

In a time when the skulls of executed criminals were powerful draw cards for phrenological lectures,[74] Hamilton incorporated examples from the gallows not only of Maitland. His collection also included the skull of a convicted Tasmanian criminal known as the 'Bagdad Murderer',[75] and in New Zealand he attended the execution of five Maoris convicted of multiple murders.[76] By the time of his death, Hamilton had collected some 55 skulls or parts thereof – about 30 Aboriginal, four Maori, one 'Hindoo', one Chinese, and the rest European.[77] He sourced them not only through grave robbing. Three of his Tasmanian criminals were all hanged and dissected, two of them at St Mary's Hospital, a 60-bed institution for the labouring classes run by the City of Hobart's medical officer Dr Samuel Edward Bedford.[78] To obtain them, Hamilton must have established personal relationships within Hobart's anatomical networks. The absences in the numbering system in the Hamilton collection today indicates that he may have traded or sold some of his skulls through these trading connections (to be discussed further in Chapter Four). Jill Dimond, biographer of Hamilton's third wife, has posited that Hamilton may even have collected the skull of Ned Kelly, as he was present when the death mask was taken.[79] However, Kelly's postcranial remains, buried in 2013, include a small L-shaped section of skull, and none of the skulls in the present-day Hamilton collection are missing such a fragment.[80] Furthermore, Hamilton's delight in public provocation makes it unlikely that he would have stayed silent about such a prize, even though the authorities were clamping down on spectacles surrounding Kelly memorabilia in the months following the execution, as Dimond illustrates.[81]

While criminals were particularly well represented among the Europeans, the Hamilton collection also included a "highly cultivated medical man", and a European-English person who "portrays character of the race – striking contrast to Aboriginals of these colonies".[82] We can speculate whether Hamilton had collected these skulls with a view to the comparitive role they would play among the heads of deviates and individuals from other races as examples of the civilised type, or whether their presence was the result of an obsession that began with an objectification of 'the other' but turned into a desire to possess any skull at any price.

A showman on trial

The charges laid against Hamilton for inciting another person to exhume corpses from a burial ground were reported across the Australian colonies, attention undoubtedly heightened by the grotesque and unusual nature of the charges.[83]

Hamilton chose to represent himself at trial. The *Sydney Morning Herald* devoted some 5,500 words to the proceedings, with 4,000 of them paraphrasing the phrenologist's defence, which provides hints of a bombastic, self-important man.[84] It is indicative of the representation of white and Aboriginal voices in the public space of the time that Windeyer's defence arguments at Jim Crow's trial were afforded just one paragraph in the case's reportage while Hamilton could claim such ample space in one of Australia's major newspapers. While we must take into account that Hamilton was arguing against conviction and possible incarceration – and could rightfully take as long as necessary to present his arguments – his choice to represent himself, and verbose manner in doing so, indicate that he may have been in his element with a jury for audience.

As with all newspaper sources, in relying on the *Herald*'s report of proceedings we must be wary of the article having passed through a journalistic filter; facts can be lost, altered or introduced.[85] However, the length of this article indicates an intention to report the trial closely, and the style of speech attributed to Hamilton correlates with his flowery wording in open letters and pamphlets.[86]

Much of Hamilton's defence was based on aspersions cast on the characters of the Reverend Greaves, the sexton House, and the church warden Ogg. Hamilton argued that he had merely enquired as to the possibility of exhuming the remains, and that House should have declined the task straight away, rather than promising to return later and instead reporting him to Greaves. Hamilton's tendency towards melodrama – a showmanship no doubt crucial to his livelihood – is evident from his colourful description of Greaves, who then "ran with the fleetness of foot of a champion pedestrian to lay the charge". The layman Ogg was said to have "contested the race of vengeance" with Greaves. It was Hamilton who was the true victim for having trusted too much in humanity and "especially upon that portion of it robed in the garments of religious teachers".

In presenting himself as a person of impeccable character, Hamilton outlined his philanthropic efforts from preceding months of lecturing. Five of his lectures, conducted across East and West Maitland and the neighbouring town of Morpeth, had raised between £5 and £23 pounds for institutions including two schools of arts, a mechanics' institute and a hospital, he claimed.

Hamilton also emphasised his position as a man of science, and argued that, just as a geologist required rocks for study, a phrenologist required skulls. He had no qualms about describing the way he had obtained the skulls in his collection – some from dissections, some received as gifts from "men high in office", and others dug up in the bush. Like the architects of Britain's *Anatomy Act*, Hamilton also attempted to play on public fears of body-snatching and murder for dissection – personified in the Irish murderers Burke and Hare who had terrorised Edinburgh to supply a medical school – to argue that the use of the bodies of criminals for anatomical studies protected the good citizen from unsavoury sorts who "might take your deceased mother, sister, child, or wife from their graves".[87] It was this kind of person whom such prosecutions should target. He also argued, somewhat bizarrely, that the great distinction between him and body snatchers was that Jones and Crow were not fresh but well decomposed after several months in the soil.

The jury found Hamilton's arguments compelling. After deliberating for just 15 minutes, they declared him not guilty. Considering the acquittal's swiftness, one might ask whether Hamilton was right in saying that it would have been simpler for House, Greaves and Ogg to simply rebuff his request verbally instead of reporting him to the police magistrate. But there must have been something highly repugnant for these men in Hamilton's attempts to retrieve skulls interred through Christian burial. Perhaps, having seen Hamilton lecture with a table of casts and skulls, they knew he would not be easily deterred. And in that fear they were correct. At some point within the next two years, Hamilton, or one of his agents, returned to St Peter's cemetery, dug up Jim Crow's body and removed the skull.

A moral puzzle

This we know because by the time he gave a phrenological lecture in Brisbane in 1862, Hamilton's lecture props featured Jim Crow. In keeping with his low view of Aboriginal intellect, he is reported to have reiterated the earlier viewpoint he gave on the cast of Jim Crow's head in 1860 (mentioned in Chapter Two): "the animal powers were very prominent, and the general development ... such as to show that the man was a complete idiot".[88]

What kind of person would return to a grave to retrieve a skull under these circumstances? Arguably, a man with an almost pathological level of self-confidence in the grip of an obsession. But can we cast Hamilton as a wholly dark figure? Unfortunately, none of Hamilton's personal papers were found during the course of my research, denying us a first-hand account of his collecting practices, and just one of his letters passed through my hands. But Hamilton left deep tracks through the colonial newspapers of Australia and New Zealand, from which we can start to build the picture of a morally ambiguous figure.

The exhumation of Jim Crow's skull was not Hamilton's only legal or social transgression. In 1865, the phrenologist caused scandal when he abruptly departed Adelaide, leaving debts unpaid.[89] In 1866, in New Zealand, he was charged with stealing plaster casts of the heads of three executed murderers that he claimed to have assisted in creating (the case was dismissed, even though Hamilton admitted to the act).[90] In 1871, Hamilton was horsewhipped in a Launceston street by a Mr Deane. Some sources alleged this was payback for insulting a lady during a lecture, others claimed a provocation from 17 years earlier.[91] Deane was ordered to pay a fine of £5 and, immediately after payment, "inquired of the Bench if he were now at liberty to horsewhip [the] complainant again at the same price".[92]

His romantic life was similarly sordid. Hamilton married three times, fulfilling the adage of the man who grows older while his women remain the same age. At the time of his first marriage to Emma Elizabeth Joscelyne in London in 1853, Hamilton was in his early thirties, while his wife was still "a minor", probably about 18.[93] When he married Adelaide-born Emily Ellis in Ballarat in 1864, Hamilton was in his mid forties, while Emily was 18.[94] By 1878, when he married his amanuensis and secretary, Agnes Melville, in Sydney, he was in his late fifties, while she was a slightly more respectable 25.[95] No children were born from any of the unions, implying either that these were sexless marriages or that Hamilton was sterile.

We can guess that his showman's presence may have drawn these much younger women to Hamilton, a charisma not immediately evident from the tufty figure in his photograph. After all, as an itinerant lecturer, Hamilton would not have been able to offer financial stability. But his relationship with his much younger wives also reflects the patriarchal power dynamics of the Victorian era, in spite of the proto-feminist mother who raised him and taught him his craft.

A particularly aching insight into these dynamics is offered within the documents of the divorce proceedings instigated by Emma Elizabeth Hamilton in 1871, proceedings brought partly on the grounds of his bigamous marriage to Emily Ellis, and we can wonder whether this event related to Hamilton's public horsewhipping.[96] Emma Elizabeth had left Hamilton shortly after they arrived in Launceston in 1854, just a year into their union. The separation was the final event in a series of acts that included Hamilton "frequently abusing her in the most violent and disgusting language", striking her "several times in the face with a large book", threatening her "with personal violence and on three occasions pour[ing] a jug of cold water over her", and striking her "in the face with his fist". On their voyage to Australia aboard *The Potentate*, the phrenologist

> pinched her violently causing great pain and on several occasions shut her up in her cabin from six o'clock in the evening until bedtime and would not allow her to have a light and threatened [her] with personal violence if she spoke to her mother or the other passengers.[97]

The one letter penned by Hamilton that I found in the course of my research hides within the Hamilton v Hamilton divorce file. Writing 17 years after the violent events, his tone is respectful, almost a little chatty, and implies that Hamilton took steps to release his first wife from their marriage. The intervening years had brought to Tasmania, among other things, the *Matrimonial Causes Act* of 1860, which brought the dissolution of marriage within the means of men and women of the working and middle classes.

I have come to Launceston to give you an opportunity of using the means at your command for a divorce from me if you are inclined to do so.

I find that you still bear my name and that you are much respected. I have seen many friends of yours of both sexes who are also friends towards me.

A few months ago I spent a few happy days at Jellelabad [sic] the residence of Mr Thomas Dowling. The Misses Dowling and Mrs J Cumming know you well. I told them I meant to visit Launceston and I expect to meet their friends in a day or two. I shall deliver a course of lectures here in the Hall of the Mechanics Institute and shall remain a few weeks for private practice.

Should you not feel inclined to take any action in the matter to which I have referred you will kindly let me know – should you express a desire that I should avoid making my name public here, I shall respect your wish [and] leave Launceston and travel at once to Hobart Town where I will do well professionally.

I shall take it kind if you give me an audience of a few minutes at your leisure.

In view of the letter's cordiality, we might wonder whether the acts of violence described by Emma Elizabeth in her petition were perhaps exaggerated, designed to bolster the likelihood of the divorce being granted or to disguise a much more impulsive catalyst for her separation – cold feet. By establishing the phrenologist's villainy as the reason for her departure, these claims might also be read as insulation against the public censure that women often suffered when, as Penny Russell explains, personal relations were exposed "to an unsympathetic public gaze".[98] While it could be presumed that the court would grant the divorce on the unequivocal fact of Hamilton's bigamy, in the hands of gossipy scribes, a husband might be forgiven for seeking happiness elsewhere if his young wife had callously left him on a whim. In fact, writes historian Ginger Frost, the mores of the period rendered bigamy relatively acceptable, and commonplace, among the working and middle classes if the spouse who remarried was seen as the wronged party.[99] However, in weighing up the validity of Emily's claims, we should also consider that, in a time when marriage equated with a woman's respectability, a decision to leave a husband was not undertaken lightly, and Emma Elizabeth probably therefore had strong cause to do so.

The even tone of Hamilton's letter reveals no sense of responsibility for the breakdown of his first marriage, although perhaps it is incorrect to apply contemporary values to expect a man of that period to reflect on his behaviour, or to empathise with what Emma Elizbeth's experience may have been. In fact, the final lines of his letter imply his own sense of loss and resignation caused by recent traumas, including Emily's departure after seven years of marriage.

> My mother is dead & my connection with one who took my name is entirely & forever severed, therefore I am prepared for all consequences: I can be the only sufferer.[100]

We can wonder at a man who described himself as "the only sufferer" in a relationship marred by alleged violence. Certainly, this sentence calls to mind the melancholy expression that Hamilton wears in his only photo, and which may have been taken during this period. The phrenologist had lost the two women in his life and was undoubtedly feeling sorry for himself. While one might entertain the possibility that "I can be the only sufferer" is a gallant invitation for his first wife to take all steps necessary to secure the divorce, this idea is negated in view of Hamilton's other transgressions and their suggestion of a blind self-confidence.

For example, his suggestion to the sexton House that he exhume Jim Crow's remains by moonlight indicates that he recognised the act's illegality. However this knowledge obviously did not trump what he felt was his right to the remains, and after the ignominy of the exhumation trial, he certainly had no qualms about returning to Maitland to unsuccessfully run for office in 1863 and 1874.[101] His defence to the charges of stealing the plaster casts in New Zealand in 1866 hinged on what he claimed to be moral rights, but his course of action, rather than negotiation or even a legal appeal, was to simply visit the office where they were stored to remove them.[102] In fact, his third wife, Agnes Hamilton, described him in her memoirs as "yielding to no one in his belief in what he professed".[103]

This bullish self-belief sits logically alongside Hamilton's collecting practices and his macabre, casual approach to death (which will be discussed more closely in the next chapter). Labels were glued directly onto many of the skulls. On the brow of one of the Maori skulls he wrote 'Memento Mori'; on another, "Oh! Man.... Dust to dust, Ashes to Ashes".[104]

The cleverest man in Australia?

While the gory aspects of Hamilton's collecting dominate his record, there is also evidence of a powerful charm. In the lead up to Hamilton's first lectures conducted upon arrival in Australia in 1854, the Hobart *Courier* wrote that "we have been made aware of Mr. Hamilton's astonishing success as a lecturer", and the *Colonial Times* commented that "if he deserves half the econium [sic] [his British Critics] would give him, he must be very well acquainted with the subject".[105] Being a great self-promoter, it is possible that Hamilton supplied this information to the newspaper himself, but the comments accord with later reports of his style being "amusing and entertaining", "felicitous", and capable of eliciting "roars of laughter".[106] In March 1860, Hamilton gave a lecture near Maitland "filled almost to suffocation. When you looked around to see if the windows were open, you found the open spaces filled with heads anxiously observing and listening".[107]

That he could forge personal connections was evidenced by a poignant encounter on the gallows in New Zealand in 1866, when Hamilton attended the execution of five Maori men associated with the Pai Marire resistance movement. Hamilton had examined the heads of the men prior to execution and – when awaiting death in the gaolyard – the Maori prophet Horomona Poropiti held out his hand to the phrenologist as his final act.[108]

Hamilton's third wife, Agnes Hamilton (later known as Agnes Hamilton-Grey), described her husband as "a mastermind in his profession", and said that she had overheard him referred to as the "cleverest man in Australia". In her memoirs, written in 1920 as an introduction to one of her biographies on the Australian poet Henry Kendall, she reflects on Hamilton's personal qualities, that "he was boyish in his sympathy with either sickness or helplessness, but he hated the liar, the trickster, the seducer of women, & the deserter of children".[109] Yet these impressions were written in the 1920s, decades after Hamilton's death in 1884, and spring from the pen of a conscious redactor of past events. The bigamy, the abuse of Emma Elizabeth and the grave robbing are all pithily captured by Agnes in an admission that "he had his faults".[110] This urge to gloss over the negative attributes of the men in her life is perhaps most explicitly captured in the work on her great intellectual obsession. She defended her verbose praise of Kendall by echoing the truism that one should not speak ill of the dead.

> Kendall may have had faults... therefore I have not tried
> to make a divine creature of him, but what I have said is

true. Surely it is better, if possible, to praise than to blame, especially when the one we write of is now where both his weaknesses & his strength will meet 'righteous' judgment.

The historian is cautioned to understand Agnes Hamilton's favourable account of her husband as fundamentally problematic. This passage about Hamilton is therefore not simply an impression penned half-a-lifetime after she was widowed; it is *impressionistic* in its evocation of a rose-tinted mood and in its blurring of detail.

Still, Agnes Hamilton is not the only person to list the phrenologist's redeeming qualities, with newspapers reports from the day offering other insights, particularly into his philanthropy. Throughout his time in Australia, Hamilton often contributed a portion of proceeds from his lectures to local charitable organisations.[111] In 1855, for example, he is also noted as having donated £13 and 10 shillings to support the British effort in the Crimean War, the equivalent of about £1,035 in today's value.[112]

But the greatest contradiction of Hamilton's character lies in his political campaigning for causes that we would today associate with small-l liberalism. While Hamilton publicly classed Aboriginal people as an inferior type, he also condemned the anti-Chinese sentiment growing on the goldfields during the 1860s.[113] He expressed this view at a public meeting in Sydney in 1861 that followed the Lambing Flat Riots, during which a white mob attacked Chinese prospectors and their property.[114] The *Maitland Mercury* cites Hamilton as causing an uproar in the room when he "denounced 'the ruffians who made the cowardly attack on the Chinese'".[115] When campaigning for office two years later, he declared that "there was a certain indirect amount of good derivable from the presence of the Chinese in the colony".[116]

Like many of his phrenological contemporaries, Hamilton also fiercely campaigned for the abolition of capital punishment. In the high-profile case of two men sentenced to death for robbing the gold escort in 1862, he circulated a petition and collected 15,000 signatures pleading for the sentence to be commuted.[117] His arguments were many-pronged. Firstly, he argued that phrenology could be used correctively in criminals. Hamilton had visited mental asylums in Britain and observed the benefits to "those poor imbeciles" by the "enlightened application of physiological science"; if such techniques could improve the mentally deficient, could they not be used on criminal minds?[118] To ignore the benefits of science was to pursue legalised brutality, he argued in an 1866 pamphlet, and thus breed it among the criminal classes.[119] Underlying his case was an appeal to human compassion. As he wrote lyrically in 1863: "When the stern letter of the law is modified on behalf of mercy to the criminal, humanity rejoices in the triumph of benevolence... it harmonises with the moral law as written in the constitution of man."[120] Finally, he also said it was morally repugnant for the state to execute individuals such as Jim Crow, whom he had shown to be intellectually deficient. He used a cast of Jim Crow's head to illustrate this argument at a Newcastle lecture not long after the execution:

> England is more merciful to her idiots, and it was reserved for New South Wales ... to put to death, in the name of law, a being so irresponsible to the moral law as this; a being without hope, without conscience, or any of those faculties that light up and adorn the mind.[121]

How do we reconcile these campaigns – thoroughly modern by many standards – with his denigration of Aboriginal people? What do we say of a phrenologist who bonded with a condemned Maori man when we know that there came to be four Maori skulls in his collection and that one of these could be that same man? Perhaps the most favourable picture is that of a charismatic man with intentions of social reform who embraced many of the common racial beliefs of the time. His contempt for authority correlated with his grave robbing and – in the case of the casts – theft. Hamilton offers a clue to the contradictions of character in 1866 when defending his earlier attempts to exhume Jim Crow's skull in a letter to a New Zealand newspaper.[122] He claimed he had intended to send it to his brother-in-law in England, "that he might get a likeness put in the *Illustrated London News*, to show the British people what kind of a creature they thought it right to hang in New South Wales".[123]

Yet we know that Hamilton never sent the skull to England, and the claim certainly does not reflect his argument at trial in 1860, when he said that he required it for scientific purposes. There are also inconsistencies in the New Zealand letter in terms of the philanthropic contributions he lists, with the £13 he donated in Hobart in 1855 for the Crimean war effort having grown to be "above twenty pounds".[124] One could of course find reasons for all of these inconsistencies: at trial, he may have calculated that an anti-capital punishment stance would be detrimental; with the passing of 11 years he may have forgotten the exact amount donated in Hobart. But taken together, the inconsistencies accumulate to reflect a talent for puffery.

Could it be that Hamilton's anti-capital punishment campaigning, with its high-profile confrontation of authority, was simply a way for him to attract public attention? His philanthropic work a way to ingratiate himself with the communities he visited? We might even ask whether Hamilton truly believed in the tenets of phrenology, or whether it was simply a convenient tool with which he could transcend his heredity as a weaver's son and become a man of science. British historian of science John van Wyhe has posited that phrenology has too frequently been described as a reform science, when it also served as a foil for the egos of the men who earned a living from it.[125] His case study for this argument is the first great populiser of phrenology, Johann Gaspar Spurzheim, who had written to his future wife: "I do what I can, in order to make me known and to acquire reputation' and 'I wish to be able to make money by the doctrine where this is possible".[126] The phrenological system, writes Wyhe, bestowed "firm and certain knowledge" and therefore social standing from which popular phrenologists could intervene in any number of reform debates.[127]

The true Hamilton may therefore lie somewhere between the polarised possibilities within the evidence: neither a sociopathic charlatan, nor a laudably well-meaning political activist and philanthropist with a penchant for exhumation. Perhaps the most stable characteristic we could attribute to him is that of showman. In lieu of a phrenological reading, and without any personal notes, we can rely only on a trail of newspaper references and advertisements. Perhaps, as one gossipy, unnamed journalist from Empire suggested in 1873, his flaws – whatever their magnitude – were pathological, and "the learned phrenologist was himself deficient in a useful bump or two".[128]

Chapter Four

Mrs Hamilton Presents a Collection

On 13 March 1889, a widow in Darlinghurst, Sydney, sat down to write a letter. While other residents of the colonial capital may have been preparing for a night of drama with 'The Last Days of Pompeii' (a "Magnificent and Realistic Spectacular" at Phillip Park), debating the impending demise of the half-sovereign, or tut-tutting over the sad case of Mrs Porteous who sought a divorce from her husband Robert after years of sustained physical abuse, Agnes Hamilton had other things on her mind.[1]

It was five years since 'effusions on the brain' had claimed the life of her husband, the itinerant phrenologist AS Hamilton. And that intervening time had not been kind. Despite Mrs Hamilton's soft beauty – large entreating eyes and curls that might invite an artist to draw her in pastel – at 35 her long-held ambitions of becoming a dramatic actress were seemingly no closer to realisation than when she had first disclosed them to Archibald in the mid 1870s.[2] For at least a brief time, she had tried to capitalise on the phrenological knowledge gleaned from her late husband and mentor, advertising her services in the *Sydney Morning Herald* just 12 days after his death in 1884.[3] But that endeavour appears to have been short lived, and she was later advised on how she might earn a living by contributing to newspapers "on feminine subjects", lecturing "at ladies's schools or colleges" or by reading aloud in French.[4] According to Jill Dimond, who has written a brief biography of Agnes Hamilton, in the years following AS Hamilton's death, she had also given birth to an illegitimate daughter, who did not survive beyond early childhood. And then there was the matter of the mysterious addendum to her surname that had turned her into Agnes Hamilton-Grey, despite there being no record of a marriage to a man of this name.[5]

On this mild autumn day, Agnes was constructing a proposal to the Board of Trustees of the Public Library, Museums and National Gallery of Victoria regarding the remnants of her husband's career, a collection that included Jim Crow.

> If you would be willing to give the skulls of the late AS Hamilton, Phrenologist, a place among the Exhibits of the above named Institution as a Phrenological Collection, I should be happy to send them to you without delay...

> The Collection of fifty 50 skulls comprises two 2 Tasmanians (last of the race) Victorian aboriginals, those also of New South Wales, Queensland, South Australia & New Zealand, Hindoo skulls and remarkable criminals and murderers – and, apart from this scientific use in the demonstrations of phrenology, are an interesting study, as they have all been selected because of their varied and peculiar physiognomy.[6]

This was the first of three letters penned by Agnes Hamilton regarding the collection's donation to the body that oversaw Melbourne's four key cultural institutions. Her missives are the starting point for reconstructing the purposes that the skull of Jim Crow served after Hamilton's death. An object has no say in who handles it, and records at Museum Victoria, as well as in associated archives, demonstrate how changing intellectual currents can wash over a deceased person in a museum collection. In 1889, Hamilton's influence was already fading from memory, but over the coming decades, his skulls would come within the ambit of new racial sciences of which he never could have dreamed.

Jim Crow steams south

Within a fortnight of her first letter, Agnes Hamilton received a favourable reply from Victoria. Almost immediately she began packing the skulls and skull fragments, although she feared that her work was "rather clumsy".[7] The numbers that appear on the yellowed labels on many of the skulls, and which are usually also inked onto the parietal bone, indicate that originally there were up to 56 skulls in this collection (some numbers duplicate). But only 47 of them made it to the museum, along with cranial fragments. Had Agnes Hamilton already sold the more interesting remains? Or was it her husband who had traded, lost or sold them during his travels?

From the scant reference in the correspondence to the process of preparing the collection, we cannot be sure what Agnes Hamilton felt as she wrapped these surviving travelling companions of her late husband – revulsion, relief, pride or affection. I have seen and handled much of the collection that Agnes Hamilton packed 125 years ago in Sydney in my capacity as a research assistant at Museum Victoria. Such handling by researchers without a cultural connection to ancestral remains is necessary in the search for clues – labels or other markings – that might ultimately enable repatriation, and at all times I worked alongside the Collections Manager for Restricted Collections. The cumulative impact of the Hamilton remains is sometimes heartbreaking, sometimes chilling. The cranial bones of children that Hamilton used as lecture props are egg-shell light, and seem too fragile to have survived more than a century in a box. Several of the adult skulls have been sliced in two, with one of them now reduced to just its bottom half.[8] A section of forehead has been sawed from the skull of convicted murderer Charles Marshall. Most of them are signed 'AS Hamilton – Phrenologist' in blue ink at the rear base of the skull, as one might inscribe a book to mark ownership. And Agnes Hamilton would have handled other, equally tragic remains that

I did not – the two Tasmanians whom she refers to as "the last of the race", or the Maori skull with tattooed skin still attached.[9] While these details are disturbing to contemporary researchers, the phrenologist's widow seemed to possess an easy familiarity with the collection. In her third letter to the museum, they became simply "the poor old skulls", leading one to wonder just how closely she had shared quarters with them over the years.[10] In some contexts, the word "poor" might indicate sympathy for the deceased, but Agnes Hamilton was here dealing with human remains as objects; if anything, the word bizarrely anthropomorphised that which had been stripped of personhood. By describing them as examples of "varied and peculiar physiognomy", she positioned herself as a learned woman unruffled by the macabre. In her third letter, she expressed regret to the Board of Trustees "that it was not in my power to send the collection to you with all the artistic accompaniments of decorum & elegance due to science".[11]

With the skulls packed, along with the fragments, phrenological charts, and even a crude, weighty brain model, Agnes Hamilton arranged for the collection to be loaded onto the Steam Ship Konoowarra for passage to Melbourne. "Kindly let me know if you receive them without breakage, as I was obliged to pack them myself," she explained to the Board of Trustees.[12] That they ever arrived at all may seem a small miracle considering that just a few days earlier the Konoowarra had run aground in Moreton Bay, with the Marine Board of Queensland later finding that "the navigation of the vessel was conducted in a very slovenly manner."

> There is no chart-room on the 'Konoowarra', and the third mate, whose watch it was, and who has … frequently visited this port, stated that he had never seen a chart of Moreton Bay… The Board consider it imperative that steamers… should be supplied with thoroughly efficient compasses of the most approved type, which is certainly not the case with this vessel.[13]

But no such dramas would impede the passage of the skulls to the southern city. And with the logistics taken care of, Agnes Hamilton began searching through her husband's papers for the catalogue that explained the collection's ethnological value. To the contemporary researcher, this document would be priceless, but Agnes Hamilton was defeated by the "hopeless chaos of manuscript left by the late erratic Professor". Instead, she included "papers giving particulars of the skulls of the late AS Hamilton… copied from rough notes dictated by himself some short time before his illness".[14]

Within one month, Agnes Hamilton had divested herself of a collection that she had stewarded for five years. We do not know her motivations for so rapidly disposing of the skulls, but could speculate that financial hardship and the loss of a child might have caused her to reflect with nostalgia on her marriage to the Scottish phrenologist, and spurred her into considering the best way to deal with his legacy. Despite their 34-year age difference, the couple appeared to have been glued together through a shared sense of theatre and self-promotion. While Archibald Hamilton revelled in the spotlight cast by chairing a protest meeting against Ned Kelly's death sentence, his third wife was herself not averse to causing a fracas by turning up to a public event costumed as a nun, as she did in Ballarat in 1882.[15] In 1930, Agnes wrote a will requesting that all of her estate be directed towards the republication of her books on the poet Henry Kendall and to their circulation to "every Parliamentary Library, every University Library, every Public and Municipal Library in the leading cities in Australia, Tasmania and New Zealand" – a posthumous expression of her dedication to Kendall, as well as her comfort with the limelight.[16]

Something of a more pressing nature may also have contributed to Agnes Hamilton's urgent disposal of the remains. Dimond writes that towards the end of 1889, or in early 1890, Agnes gave birth to George, a son she argues was fathered illegitimately by future Prime Minister George Houstoun Reid, who was godfather to the boy. The key evidence pointing to paternity is in the correspondence between Agnes and Reid's friend AB Piddington regarding the Form of Information submitted for obtaining a death certificate after George Hamilton-Grey's untimely death in 1925. Piddington refused to include 'Houston Reid' as the boy's surname as was "the practice of the Department when children are born out of wedlock".[17] Certainly, that Reid may have fathered illegitimate children is possible if we refer to his biographer Winston Gregory McMinn who describes him as "a bon vivant, and also, from all accounts, a ladies' man".[18] If this birth occurred in the earlier part of the timeframe posited by Dimond – late 1889 – Agnes might already have known about the pregnancy when she wrote her letter to Melbourne. The donation of the skulls could therefore have constituted an attempt to clear out elements of her former life to make a fresh start in raising her then unborn child. Perhaps the father of her child was jealous of these relics of her husband. Or, perhaps the stress of being the 'other woman' in Reid's life invoked a yen for the period when she herself was married and therefore enjoyed greater legitimacy.

A more prosaic reason might also explain this delay in donation: perhaps Agnes Hamilton had attempted to donate her collection to other museums and been rejected. The archives of other leading institutions of the time such as the Australia Museum may reveal similar letters that begin with the *pro forma* address of 'Gentlemen'.[19]

Whatever her motivation, Agnes Hamilton's first letter to the Board of Trustees leaves little doubt that the donation was intended to memorialise the work of her late husband, and to carve a place for phrenology within a formal institutional context. Agnes was a consummate donor, conveying the bulk of her Kendall manuscripts and photographs, as well as some personal papers, to the Mitchell Library prior to her death wrapped in annotated brown paper packages.[20] In her letter presenting the skulls, she was quick to emphasise the altruistic impulses for the gift.

It may be as well to state that I have no pecuniary interest in making it a condition of the gift that the skulls be accepted as a Phrenological Collection, as since my husband's death I have not practised the science either as a delineator of character or as a lecturess.[21]

In her third and final letter, Agnes Hamilton also envisaged an educational role for the collection, asking that the skulls be given "such a position in your museum as would enable them to tell their own phrenological story to the earnest and benevolent enquiries".[22] The request of course was cleverly angled to secure recognition for Hamilton himself: what renders the story of each skull within the collection 'phrenological' is chiefly the phrenologist himself, and Agnes Hamilton might have expected that his name would become attached to this particular museum display. There is a macabre symmetry in this vision of the deceased AS Hamilton continuing to live through the exhibition of these dead men and women through whom he had earned his living. But the reality of what happened to the collection once it arrived in Melbourne would end up being quite different to the hopes of the phrenologist's widow.

Marvellous science in thriving Melbourne

For the six years of their marriage between 1878 and 1884, the Hamiltons toured and lectured in Sydney and across Victoria, and during this time Agnes Hamilton may have forged the connections to the city that prompted her to consider donating to one of the Melbourne museums. These were thriving times for knowledge and discovery in the southern colony. The many decades of affluence reaped from the Victorian goldfields during the mid-nineteenth century had been expressed to the rest of the colonies, and to the world, through a series of high-profile exhibitions in 1866–67, 1880 and 1888, events that showcased Australia's cultural and technological advancements.[23] Intertwined with this exhibition movement were the National Museum of Victoria, the Industrial and Technological Museum, the Public Library and the National Gallery of Victoria, which were brought together under one Board of Trustees in 1870.

In 1889, all of these institutions, except the National Museum of Victoria, shared a series of spaces behind the neo-classical portico on Melbourne's Swanston Street, today still the site of the State Library of Victoria. This warren of galleries and stacks housed manuscripts and objects ranging from the classics, to the rules and regulations of the Clifton Hill Temperance Fire Brigade, to displays of ethnographic art and coins, to oil paintings and sculptures, and to rocks and minerals gleaned from across Australia.[24] Artistic young men and women of the right sort took drawing classes with the artist Frederick McCubbin. Until a decade prior, those of a more practical bent had enrolled in courses in the emerging technology of telegraphy.[25] Slightly north of this site was the National Museum of Victoria, overseen by Frederick McCoy, who had moved the collections to the University of Melbourne in 1856.[26]

This period also saw the bloom of the dynamic new field of ethnography, with the intrepid contributions of Alfred William Howitt in Victoria among the most famous examples. The fact that the discipline was still emerging in the late nineteenth century is reflected in the way that the terms 'ethnographic', 'ethnological' and 'ethnotypical' are used more or less interchangeably within the early annual reports of the Board of Trustees. But it would not be until Walter Baldwin Spencer took custody of the National Museum of Victoria in 1899, and discovered his love for the successor field to ethnography – anthropology – that human remains in Melbourne would become central to understanding the Indigenous body.

For most of the nineteenth century, the trade in human remains was propelled by the medical fraternity, comparative anatomists, and proponents of cranial 'sciences' such as phrenology. In view of this intellectual climate, and of the individual personalities of the major players within the institutions, the Hamilton collection's destination is unexpected by contemporary standards. The National Museum, with its natural history focus, may today seem like the logical place to have received human remains. Its director, Frederick McCoy, was a leading comparative biologist and critic of Darwin, and had taught anatomy at the University of Melbourne. But his relationship with Aboriginal remains and artefacts was fraught, compared to other life forms, a fact hinted at by the jokes of his medical students about McCoy's love of the sea sponge.[27] Some human skulls were listed in an inventory of the museum's collections that appeared in the 1875 annual report, and their display in the cabinets is evident from sources including an opinion article in *The Argus* in 1868, and an 1891 piece in *Speculum* (the newspaper of the University of Melbourne medical students).[28] But historian Gareth Knapman argues that McCoy saw "ethnology [as] being in the domain of art", and speculates that any human remains in McCoy's care would have been a legacy from the varied collections that contributed to the birth of the National Museum in 1854.[29] In fact, writes Knapman, McCoy was often given first pick of ethnographic objects that he then diverted to the library or the gallery.[30]

One therefore has to look elsewhere for ethnography among these four institutions. From 1873, the annual reports list a so-called Ethnotypical Museum as falling within the operations of the National Gallery of Victoria. In 1874, the ethnological collection was under the stewardship of the landscape artist Eugene von Guerard, who fulfilled multiple functions but was primarily the instructor of painting for the Gallery.[31] Initially, these ethnological goods were limited to objects and 'curios', but by the 1880s, the donations also included human skulls, generally as part of larger groups of artefacts arriving from one location or expedition. For example, a collection donated in 1885 from New Guinea included coconut water bottles, native weapons, paddles and human skulls.[32] Human remains were also acquired to fulfill unexpected functions, such as the skeleton obtained in 1878 for the drawing classes organised by the Gallery.

The Industrial and Technological Museum (ITM) was originally established to foster appreciation of the applied sciences and technologies generated by an industrialising Britain. During the 1870s it received a number of "native" artefacts that correlated with its collecting focus on the products of human industry.[33] In 1886, the ITM would assume greater control of the ethnography collections, when its glamorously named superintendent, J Cosmo Newbery (the owner of a luxurious moustache that jutted alertly past his cheeks), began managing them in tandem with the director of the National Gallery, the portraitist George Frederick Folingsby.[34]

The annual reports of the many-headed hydra that was the Board of Trustees are available online, but other documentation – minute books, letter registers and correspondence – are scattered across multiple Melbourne sites.[35] All incoming correspondence to the Board was serialised by diligent nineteenth-century clerks, who attached a cover sheet and entered them alphabetically into leather-bound registers that today crumble over the white cotton gloves of those who peruse them. Sometimes entire years of the actual correspondence are missing, but the overall order inspires respect for these exacting secretaries, including for the person who entered the words "Offers to present collection of skulls" alongside the name of Agnes Hamilton in the inward letter register of 1889.[36] In scribbled ink and pencil, the cover page of her first letter reveals the negotiations over who should take custody of this singular collection.

The letter was first referred to Newbery, who deemed it "an interesting collection" but left the question of whether it would be a 'phrenological' collection to the chair of the Board's technical committee, government astronomer Robert 'Bob' LJ Ellery."[37] From his base at the Melbourne Observatory, Ellery declared that it should be accepted, "but the aboriginal and other national specimens will be most in place as a part of ethnology". Before Hamilton's life work had even arrived at the museum, it was to be split up, contravening Agnes Hamilton's requests that the skulls be regarded as a discrete phrenological grouping. This letter also explains one of the enduring mysteries for researchers at Museum Victoria: why different parts of the collection were registered more than half a century apart. The cover sheet of Agnes Hamilton's third letter, in which she included notes to the collection, tells us that it was forwarded to Oliver Rule, Curator of Mineral Collections and Instructor in Practical Mineralogy at the ITM from 1878.[38] As an employee of Newbery, he may have been delegated the task of looking after the ethnographic collection, a hypothesis supported by notes on the cover sheet of another ethnographic collection that arrived from New Zealand later in 1889.[39]

At this point, the paper trail is interrupted for more than a decade. It was not until the early twentieth century, several years after the ethnographic collections were brought under the steward-ship of Baldwin Spencer at the National Museum of Victoria, that some of the remains within the Hamilton collection were registered.[40] Where had the collection languished until this time? Quite possibly in boxes in a back room, as the overwhelming evidence is that these were not considered a significant acquisition at the time of their donation. Rule's correspondence file in the Museum Archives, which spans from 1881 to 1891 reflects a lifelong passion for rocks and minerals, with no letters regarding ethnographic artefacts or human remains.[41] As a man who felt so ardently about geology, perhaps Rule resented being tasked with this messy discipline of people. Neither the minute books for the Industrial and Technological Museum, nor for the Board of Trustees, discuss the receipt of the collection.[42] In fact, it does not even rate a mention in the annual report for 1889, a glaring omission for a collection of this size.[43] The fact that human remains, and ethnographic collections in general, were sandwiched between the Industrial and Technological Museum and National Gallery of Victoria, may have contributed to the collection's oversight when the directors sat down to write their reports at the end of the year. The timeframes within which objects were accessioned and acknowledged during the nineteenth century were haphazard by today's museum practices.

However, this omission may also have been intentional. As discussed in the previous chapter, Hamilton had positioned himself as provocateur, vocally criticising the judiciaries and legislatures of various colonies in regard to issues ranging from the death penalty to the supply of human remains. In 1880, he had taken a central role in protests against Ned Kelly's death sentence, part of a popular movement that caused headaches for law enforcement and crowd control.[44] Nine years later, the Board of Trustees comprised men of the political elite including Sir Graham Berry, who – as Premier and member of the Executive Council in late 1880 – had upheld the death penalty meted out to Kelly by Justice Redmond Barry.[45] Barry, who himself had served as Chair of the Board of Trustees for a decade, expired just 12 days after the execution of Kelly, an event so institutionally traumatic that the museum was closed to allow for the funeral.[46] This was a society characterised by complex webs of inter-personal entanglements. When we consider Hamilton's connections with the Kelly affair and his greater array of less savoury pecadillos – grave robbing, head-cast stealing, bigamy – we might surmise that the Board was keen to disassociate itself from Mrs Hamilton's gift.

An object of new science

Jim Crow's journey south in 1889 marked the end of his travels with the phrenological Hamiltons. But now that he had metamorphosed from lecturing tool to museum piece, Crow would become one among hundreds of skulls that would eventually assist in establishing the National Museum of Victoria in the early twentieth century as a front-runner in anthropology.[47] As part of this transition, he would pass through the hands of one of Australia's most prominent practitioners of craniometry and race science.

Richard Berry (no relation to Graham Berry) arrived from Edinburgh in 1906 to take up a position as Professor of Anatomy at the University of Melbourne, and over the next twenty years on Australian soil would establish himself as the great surveyor of Melbourne's heads. His views on the volume of the human skull were turned in equal measures to the skulls of Aboriginal people and to the heads of living convicted criminals and school children.[48]

Any reader of his 1954 memoirs, *Chance and Circumstance*, might at first be charmed by the anatomist's engaging writing style, which launches from Berry's beginnings as an orphan in Lancashire, to his education in two eccentric, privately run schools that only the Victorian Era or Charles Dickens could generate, to his miserable beginnings of working life in shipping ("I now found myself apprenticed, indentured, or bound – whatever it may be called – to a firm of shipbrokers, Mssrs. Culliford, Clark & Co... I do not know whom these two gentlemen were, nor indeed if they existed"), to his impulsive decision to study medicine.[49] But this pleasure turns to discomfort as Berry slowly reveals his dark ideology – his advocacy of euthanasia for individuals termed "mental deficients", and his summers spent digging for human remains.[50]

> I am sure, that no member of my family would ever regret the many happy summer holidays we all spent together in the very beautiful island of Tasmania. That we went there at all, was due in the first place to the necessity of adding...to our scanty store of Tasmanian aboriginal material, especially skulls.[51]

In his drive to boost the university's teaching aids, which would also include remains from south-eastern Australia, Berry also often enlisted the support of his students.[52]

In 1909, Berry and collaborator AWD Robertson, a doctor and researcher in the Department of Anatomy, published a book containing sketches of Tasmanian skulls, by this time a great prize in collecting circles.[53] To execute these tracings they employed a dioptrograph, a box-like device into which the skull would be clamped to allow for accuracy in sketching its dimensions.[54] The aim of these pictures – which really show the merest outline of the cranial bones and ridges in each person – was to allow the community of physical anthropologists around the world to add otherwise inaccessible remains to their data sets. *The British Medical Journal* applauded their contribution:

> Drs. Berry and Robertson have discovered, or, at least, are the first to describe, no less than 42 Tasmanian crania, of which only 2 are characterized as fragmentary. Of 78 crania of that race previously known and described, 3 were fragmentary; we have, therefore, an addition of 40 good specimens to our previous stock of 75, or more than one-third of the total number. Eleven of these 42 appear to have been actually discovered and disinterred by Drs. Berry, Robertson, and Crowther, of Hobart.[55]

Although some critics argued that the volume should have included interpretations of the tracings by the authors, Robertson and Berry's Tasmanian volume was overall received with such excitement that they followed with a monograph on Aboriginal skulls from South-Eastern Australia, published in 1914.[56] These two volumes were later described by Harry Brookes Allen, Professor of Pathology at the University of Melbourne, as among the greatest achievements of the medical school.[57]

Ninety skulls were traced for 'Dioptrographic Tracings in Three Normae of Ninety Australian Aboriginal Crania', including 52 from the National Museum of Victoria, and eight from the Hamilton collection. This was 'science' supported at the highest level, with the successive Victorian Premiers John Murray and William Alexander Watt both acknowledged in the introduction for their roles in assisting the 1909 and 1914 monographs.

> It must be as gratifying to these gentlemen as it is to us to see that their public spirited action in this matter has been recorded in the pages of [the journal] *L'Anthropologie*, as furnishing an example to the Governments of the civilized world.[58]

Yet this published iteration of Berry's great civilising project contained a crucial flaw in terms of sample. Berry and Robertson claimed that, apart from six crania from Queensland, the skulls were "a homogenous collection from a region south of the Murray River".[59] Physical anthropologists today know just how diverse groups can be, even within a limited region such as Victoria. The inclusion of six skulls from northern Australia in a sample of southern remains therefore seems bizarre, although perhaps understandable when we consider that Berry and Robertson were attempting to convey this data to distant researchers, and that each tracing would be greedily received by readers. But there is a clearer error here that is pertinent to our story: listed among the skulls examined at the National Museum of Victoria was X13001, the skull of Jim Crow. In fact two blue marks at the rear base of Jim Crow's skull are likely to have served as datum points for this dioptrographic task.

It is ironic that Jim Crow, who would later be misidentified as a woman from Victoria in the late twentieth century, had already been misclassified a hundred years earlier as a resident of Victoria. Yet any human turned into a museum object is vulnerable to such destabilisation of identity; the very act of collection in such contexts of grave-robbing denies personhood. Did Berry or Robertson err in misclassifying Jim Crow as coming from south of the Murray? Did they not know that Maitland was in New South Wales? Or did they know the truth but nevertheless decide to include Jim Crow's skull in their sample?

Unfortunately, the book tells us nothing about the interaction of the two men with Jim Crow's skull. Nor does Berry's memoirs. Although the dioptrographic sketches were valuable to the scientific community in 1914, the three sketches of Crow – depicting a frontal, side and top view – offer nothing to either the lay person or contemporary researchers interested in provenance. Already reduced to registration number X13001 within the National Museum, in Berry and Robertson's book Jim Crow became simply 44. The perimeter of his skull is marked with dots and corresponding letters to explain the anatomical points on the skull (G for glabella, Br for bregma, and so forth). It is a reductive mathematics that, by comparison, makes Hamilton's language of phrenology seem oddly humanising.

This would not be the last time that the Hamilton collection and Jim Crow were objects of research. The skulls themselves bear traces of other scientists – circular stickers, chalk marks with male and female symbols – but who bestowed them is unclear. Two coin-sized sections of bone have been taken from Crow's skull, and a third such core was commenced but never completed, leaving a circular imprint.

These puncture wounds speak of another life for Jim Crow as a model on which doctors, surgeons or students practised trepanation – the medical procedure in which a small section of skull was removed to reduce pressure caused by illness or injury. Trepanation dates back thousands of years, with skulls from cultures around the world showing the telltale marks of scraping, cutting, boring and drilling. By the nineteenth and early twentieth centuries, it had become a delicate skill involving a cylindrical saw with a centering pin in the middle to hold the instrument in place.[60] Remarkably, many patients survived this procedure, even in days long before modern hygiene, a fact physical anthropologists can deduce from the softening of the circle of bone as the edges healed. By contrast, the crisp edges of the trepanations in the skull of Jim Crow indicate that the procedure was carried out after his death.[61]

These circular omissions are not depicted in *Dioptrographic Tracings*, suggesting either that they were made after the compilation of the book, or that Berry and Robertson had omitted them from their sketches as 'unnatural' additions to the skull. However, this documentary evidence of Jim Crow entering the sphere of medical academia suggests that somebody with University of Melbourne connections, perhaps even Berry himself, removed these sections. Whenever it occurred, the procedure led to the further disassembling of a man already separated from his post-cranial remains.

History unwrapped

It wasn't until the 1960s that the non-Indigenous crania from the Hamilton collection – Europeans, a 'Hindoo' skull, the two Maori omitted in the original ethnographic separation of 1889 – were even registered at the National Museum of Victoria. By this stage, phrenology had largely receded from Australian public life. For the man or woman who catalogued them, the nineteenth-century scrawl on the Hamilton labels, the string that held the bisected head of the murderer Drake together, the faded roadmap of phrenological lines on the head of an unnamed criminal that Hamilton had simply called 'No. 19' – all of these must have seemed like relics from a sideshow, a silly time when the scientific disciplines were yet to establish their own hardened boundaries.[62]

These last remains were dutifully identified in the register as part of the Hamilton collection. But the meaning of the name 'Hamilton' became confused over the years. Other remains were erroneously attributed to it – for example, some from the police station in Hamilton, western Victoria. Thus, although the name remained, the identity of the collector was misunderstood, not unlike the confusion surrounding the identity of Jim Crow or the people with whom he shares a cabinet, many of whom remain difficult to provenance.[63] The memorialising project envisaged by Agnes Hamilton when she contacted the museum in 1889 has therefore turned out to be rather different, with history a harsh judge of both the Scotsman and the practice that made him notorious. Many memories have slipped away. What became of the "hopeless chaos of manuscript" through which Agnes Hamilton riffled in search of her late husband's catalogue? Did she also donate these precious pages, which today could fill the silences within the life of AS Hamilton? Or were these burned or thrown away?

More poignantly for the work of provenancing remains, the explanatory notes that Agnes Hamilton sent to the museum with her third letter have been separated from the letter in the archives at the Public Records Office of Victoria. These might hold the key to the identities of other members of the Hamilton collection, yet my search through the museum and records at the State Library of Victoria did not uncover these bashful papers. I hope it is only a matter of time. The identity of Jim Crow, so crucial to his repatriation, took a quarter of a century of museum research to uncover, and ultimately hinged on quantum leaps in digital archiving of newspapers. I like to think that one day a folder in the archives of Museum Victoria will drop to the floor, and that delicate pages filled with Agnes Hamilton's confident handwriting will slip out of them.

For all of her purported loyalty to the strictures of science, towards the end of her life the phrenologist's widow found herself at the mercy of the spirit world. It was a series of persistent rappings that disturbed her slumbers in 1920 that prompted Agnes Hamilton to commence her first biography of Henry Kendall, a propulsion so forceful that she completed the draft in six weeks.

> I am not a spiritualist, nor was I ever one, but I must confess
> that … I had been hearing rapping's [sic] for some time

but, while, sometimes concerned about them, I generally dismissed the thought of them by supposing something was loose in my bedstead, & wrattling [sic] with certain positions of my body, or some such reasoning.[64]

On reflection, she realised that she had already been receiving communications in the 1880s, in the form of a poem by Kendall that came to her hands, and which she later included in a rousing lecture on Patriots and Patriot Bards, although she was still adamant that "I am far from being a spiritist, or spiritualist". At the time that she now recalled, a fellow lecturer in Stawell had "lent me a stone to put to my forehead to see if I had any experiences, but I had none. He asked me if I ever had visions, but I was hopeless. He thought, from my lecturing, & my eyes that I was a medium, but he was, I think, mistaken". The words "I think" had been scribbled in later, as though, three decades after this meeting, Agnes Hamilton was flirting with the idea that perhaps the other lecturer was correct regarding her gifts with the spirits, at least in Kendall's case. Yet we can wonder how she managed to wrap 47 skulls without hearing messages from any of the people from whom they were taken. These are the stories that historians now hope to hear through the trail of documents. But perhaps Agnes Hamilton was listening for rappings in all the wrong places.

Afterword: Jim Crow Found

This narrative represents only a portion of the repatriation process. While the stories of Jim Crow, AS Hamilton and Agnes Hamilton shed light on whose remains might be in the collection and how it came to be stored in a museum, the story of Jim Crow will continue to write itself as Museum Victoria works with communities from his country to meet their wishes for the return of his remains.

Not only institutions keep ancestral remains, as is highlighted by the honest account of John Danalis in his 2009 book *Riding the Black Cockatoo*. The repatriation narrative told by this Queensland author is of a skull that his family kept on their mantelpiece for decades, a Wamba Wamba man from the Murray River whom they affectionately called 'Mary'. *Riding the Black Cockatoo* documents Danalis's growing understanding of the violent history of collection, and he documents the process that led to 'Mary' being returned to country. "Dad used to lacquer the skull every so often to prevent the bone from crumbling away into chalk and, I suspect, because he enjoyed lacquering things."[1] The urge with which people hold onto objects is often irrational, the accumulation of tiny pay-offs from repeated acts, be they lacquering or measuring, that furnish us with a sense of comfort and meaning. To return Aboriginal remains is to close the door to future research on these bones, or to the strange familiarity of the family skull on the mantelpiece. And while for some researchers this is irresponsible, it is also the right thing to do.

But as this book attests, researching provenance is never easy. Since beginning this project in March 2013, I have traversed disciplines including physical anthropology to resolve fundamental questions about the gender of the skull labelled 'Jim Crow' and how it came to the Museum. I have explored the significance of the iconic name within the context of transnational racism in the nineteenth century, and also unpicked the reasons behind Archibald Sillars Hamilton's determination to collect Jim Crow. The heady events of 1860 led to two trials: one for rape, and one for inciting to exhume remains from a cemetery. The social circumstances of the defendants resulted in two starkly different processes and verdicts, determined through the viewpoints and prejudices of the all-white juries. These trials were emblematic of their time, not only reflecting the changing relations in the pastoral frontier of colonial New South Wales but also the race for knowledge about the human species and the ensuing trade in remains.

Such objectification of bones continued into the late twentieth century, long after grave robbing as mastered by Hamilton became a distant embarrassment. Museums and universities cloaked their possession of remains in scientific frameworks and sanitised laboratory spaces. Only in the last 30 to 40 years have changing attitudes opened the doorway for history to reclaim the fragments of the human subject but, by then, as demonstrated by the Hamilton collection, the papers are often misplaced, the collections having been stored in different locations, clues as to provenance hidden until such time as they choose to reveal themselves. If ever.

Looming above the many unanswered questions is this: where is the rest of Jim Crow? Because Hamilton was only interested in skulls, we can speculate that he left the postcranial remains of Jim Crow and murderer John Jones in the soil of the historical cemetery of St Peter's Church in East Maitland, disused since 1890.[2] Identifying markers such as the gate near which Jim Crow was said to be buried no longer exist, meaning that the location of his grave could today only really be determined from parish records, if these recorded the grave plots of convicted criminals. Could technology be harnessed to map out the potential burial sites of the executed men? Could it identify incomplete human remains?

Aboriginal history, disowned for so long by western historical practices and actively suppressed in the national story, will always be defined by its silences. This search has taken me in surprising theoretical directions as I constructed possibilities to fill these silences. It also physically transported me to unexpected places.

I travelled from Melbourne to Maitland in August 2013, not on a farcically ill-equipped steamship as Archibald and Agnes would have in their day, but by plane and then a hire car that cut through the pastures of the Hunter Valley. Standing in the East Maitland cemetery, I felt the eerie presence of both Jim Crow and Hamilton, could imagine the figure of the Scottish phrenologist investigating the newly turned soil that concealed the object of his obsession. In an Aboriginal sense of time, in which past and present intermingle, and in which I am the living witness to the lives of these two men, I sensed also the ghosts of future possibilities. The story I have presented here will hopefully be improved upon, completed. I hope it will allow Jim Crow to return home.

Notes

Prologue

1   For a brief description of this relationship with the police, see RTM Pescott, *Collections of a Century*, National Museum of Victoria, Melbourne, 1954, p. 96.

2   The human skull comprises the cranium (the larger, main part) and the mandible, or jaw. Jim Crow's skull does not include the mandible, and at the museum is referred to as a cranium. I have chosen to use 'skull' in this thesis, however, to reflect the vernacular of both contemporary times and the period in which Crow and Hamilton both lived.

3   *The Courier*, 30 April 1862, p. 2.

4   Michael Pickering, 'Where are the Stories?', *The Public Historian*, Vol. 32 (1), 2010, p. 81.

5   Judy Atkinson, *Trauma Trails, Recreating Song Lines: The Transgenerational Effects of Trauma in Indigenous Australia*, North Melbourne, 2003, p. 209.

6   Tom Griffiths, *Hunters and Collectors*, Oakleigh, 1996, pp. 281–282.

7   Bain Attwood, *Telling the Truth About Aboriginal History*, Crows Nest, 2005, pp. 159–160.

Chapter 1

1   Jim Crow Death Certificate, NSW Registry of Births, Deaths and Marriages, No 1860/004431. Museums Australia Inc., the industry peak body, in 2005 published *Continuous Cultures, Ongoing Responsibilities: Principles and Guidelines for Australian museums working with Aboriginal and Torres Strait Islander cultural heritage*. Section 1.4.4 (p. 18) of the document states: "Museums are to seek out the rightful custodians of ancestral

remains and ask them whether they wish the remains to be repatriated to the community".

2   An example of this conclusion can be found in the 2013 Ancillary Report on Individual x13001 by physical anthropologist Colin Pardoe, kept in the Jim Crow File, Restricted Collections, Humanities Department, Museum Victoria. I am very grateful to Colin Pardoe for providing me with materials and advice in May 2014 that helped me to better understand the thorny matter of sex determination.

3   Section 1.4.9 of *Continuous Cultures* states: "Access to … ancestral remains held by museums should be carefully controlled according to the wishes of the traditional custodians or those authorised by them". At the Museum Victoria, such requests are considered by the Aboriginal Cultural Heritage Advisory Committee.

4   This is described as a process of 'translation' by the National Museum's Michael Pickering, 'Lost in Translation', *Borderlands*, Vol. 7 (2), 2008, p. 6.

5   In 1984, the National Museum of Victoria was amalgamated with the Science Museum of Victoria to become a new organisation known as the Museum of Victoria. Its name was simplified in 1998 to Museum Victoria. Carolyn Rasmussen (ed), *A Museum for the People*, Scribe Publications, 2001, front matter.

6   Sarah Robertson, 'Sources of Bias in the Murray Black Collection: Implications for Paleopathological Analysis', *Australian Aboriginal Studies*, Vol. 1, 2007.

7   Ibid., p. 117; Cressida Fforde, *Collecting the Dead*, Duckworth, London, 2004, p. 106.

8   Shannon Faulkhead and Jim Berg (eds), *Power and the Passion: Our Ancestors Return Home*, Melbourne, 2010, p. 15.

9   Ibid., p. 17.

10 Fforde 2004, p. 89.

11 Moira Simpson, *Making Representations: Museums in the Post-Colonial Era*, Routledge, London, 1996, p. 237. The UNESCO seminar was called 'Preserving Indigenous Cultures: A New Role for Museums'.

12 Ann Kakaliouras, 'An Anthropology of Repatriation: Contemporary Physical Anthropological and Native American

Ontologies of Practice', *Current Anthropology*, Vol. 53
(Supplement 5), 2012, p. 210.

13   Fforde, 'From Edinburgh University to the Ngarrindjeri nation,
      South Australia', *Museum International*, Vol. 61 (1–2), 2009, p. 45.

14   Hilary Smale, 'Human Bones Returned for Reburial in
      Kimberley Community', ABC Online, 30 April 2013,
      http://www.abc.net.au/local/audio/2013/04/30/3748571.htm.
      Accessed 5 July 2013.

15   Larry J Zimmerman, 'A Decade after the Vermillion Accord:
      What has Changed and What has Not?' in Cressida Fforde,
      Jane Hubert, Paul Turnbull (eds), *The Dead and Their Possessions:
      Repatriation in Principle, Policy and Practice*, Routledge,
      London, 2002, pp. 91–98.

16   Martin Thomas, 'Because it's your country', *Australian
      Book Review*, April 2013. Available online: https://www.
      australianbookreview.com.au/component/k2/98-april-2013-no-
      350/1400-because-it-s-your-country. Accessed 20 May 2014.

17   *Continuous Cultures, Ongoing Responsibilities*, Section 1.4.4 and
      1.4.7, p. 18.

18   'Australian servicemen listed as missing in action in Vietnam',
      the website of the Australian War Memorial. Available at:
      http://www.awm.gov.au/encyclopedia/vietnam_mia/. Accessed
      20 May 2014.

19   Faulkhead and Berg, p. 16.

20   Cressida Fforde, Jane Hubert, Paul Turnbull (eds),
      'Introduction', in *The Dead and Their Possessions*, pp. 1–2; Roslyn
      Poignant, *Professional Savages*, UNSW Press, Sydney, 2004, p.
      242; Fforde 2004, p. 94.

21   Faulkhead and Berg, p. xx.

22   Walter Palm Island, 'Tambo', in Fforde *et al.*, p. 223.

23   Ibid., p. 225.

24   'The Australian Eleven: The First Australian Team', National
      Museum of Australia Website, http://www.nma.gov.au/
      collections/collection_interactives/cricketing_journeys/cricket_
      html/the_australian_eleven/the_australian_eleven_the_first_
      australian_team. Accessed 7 August 2013.

25   Richard Broome, *Aboriginal Victorians*, Sydney, 2005, p. 40;
      Clare Gervasoni, 'A Confusion of Tongues: overcoming

language difficulties on the Jim Crow Goldfield', in Keir
Reeves and David Nichols (eds), *Deeper Leads: New Approaches
to Victorian Goldfields History*, Ballarat Heritage Services,
Ballarat, 2007, *passim*; Edgar Morrison, 'Loddon Aborigines:
Tales of Old Jim Crow', Yandoit, 1971.

26   Richard Waterhouse, 'The Internationalisation of American
Popular Culture in the Nineteenth Century: The Case of the
Minstrel Show', *Australasian Journal of American Studies*, Vol. 4
(1), 1985, p. 1.

27   The racehorse is mentioned in *Bell's Life in Sydney and Sporting
Reviewer*, 24 July 1847, p. 1; the ship appears in *The Courier*
(Hobart), 11 July 1846, p. 4; and the criminals are referred to in
Empire, 8 October 1853, p. 5.

28   *A Pictorial History of Maitland & Morpeth*, Compiled and
Published by *The Newcastle Herald*, 1996, p. 13. The sculpture
in Narynna was carved by Tasmanian caricaturist Tom
Midwood, probably in the late nineteenth century. Although
this was some decades after Jim Crow's lifetime, the carving
nevertheless demonstrates a familiarity with US racial
archetypes in the Australian colonies.

29   See: Cassandra Pybus, *Black Founders: The Unknown Story of
Australia's First Black Settlers*, UNSW Press, Sydney, 2006.

30   Dungog blanket return, 1837, Special Bundle 4/1133.3, NSW
State Records.

31   Marilyn Wood, 'Nineteenth Century Bureaucratic
Construction of Indigenous Identities in New South Wales',
in Nicolas Peterson and Will Sanders (eds), *Citizenship and
Indigenous Australians*, Oakleigh, 1998, p. 39.

32   Dungog Blanket registers, 1837, 1838 and 1842. By contrast,
the Lake Macquarie registers, contained in Special Bundle
4/6666B.3, do not list Aboriginal names, indicating a different
attitude there.

33   Although it is difficult to see why four native men of the
NSW central coast who appear in the 1837 Dungog list
would choose to call themselves 'Bungary', the variant of a
name of a famous Aboriginal associate of Matthew Flinders
and a Sydney identity (see: FD McCarthy, 'Bungaree (?–
1830)', Australian Dictionary of Biography, National Centre
of Biography, Australian National University,

http://adb.anu.edu.au/biography/bungaree-1848/text2141. Accessed 26 September 2013.)

34   Several blank forms demonstrating this template can be found in Bundle 4/6666B.3, NSW State Records.

35   John Mathew, *Eaglehawk and Crow: A Study of the Australian Aborigines, Including an Inquiry Into Their Origin and a Survey of Australian Languages*, Mullen and Slade, Melbourne, 1899, p. 17.

36   Martin Thomas, *The Many Worlds of RH Mathews: In Search of an Australian Anthropologist*, Allen & Unwin, Sydney, 2011, p. 365.

37   Wood, p. 41.

38   John K Lundy, 'Physical Anthropology in Forensic Medicine', *Anthropology Today*, Vol. 2 (5), 1986, p. 14.

39   Pamela L Geller, 'Skeletal Analysis and Theoretical Complications', *World Archaeology*, Vol. 37 (4), 2005, p. 599; Kelly Knudson and Christopher Stojanowski, 'New Directions in Bioarchaeology: Recent Contributions to the Study of Human Social Identities', *Journal of Archaeological Research*, Vol. 16 (4), 2008, p. 400.

40   Pardoe, Ancillary Report on Individual x13001.

41   Colin Pardoe, 'Repatriation, Reburial and Biological Research in Australia: Rhetoric and Practice', in S Tarlow and L Ullman (eds), *Burial Archaeology*, Oxford University Press, Oxford, 2013, p. 733.

42   Pardoe, 'Repatriation, Reburial and Biological Research in Australia: Rhetoric and Practice', p. 744.

43   Colin Pardoe, 'Report to the Tasmanian Museum and Art Gallery', April 2014, p. 14. Supplied by the author.

44   Peter Brown, 'Sex determination of Aboriginal crania from the Murray River Valley', *Archaeology in Oceania*, Vol. 16 (1), 1981, p. 53. In making this statement, Brown cites SL Washburn, 'Sex differences in the pubic bone', *American Journal of Physical Anthropology*, Vol. 6 (2), 1948, pp. 199–208, and EA Hooton, 'Medico-legal Aspects of Physical Anthropology', *Clinics*, Vol. 1, 1943.

45   Brown, p. 53.

46   Ibid., pp. 59–60.

47   Website of Organisation Intersex International Australia, http://
       oii.org.au/19853/welcome/. Accessed 25 July 2013. 'Intersex' is
       now preferred to the term 'hermaphrodite' for describing a
       number of conditions of non-binary sexuality.

48   Geller, discussing Ann Fausto-Sterling, *Sexing the Body: Gender
       Politics and the Construction of Sexuality*, New York, 2000
       (who argues for the higher figure), and her opponent Leonard
       Sax, 'How Common is Intersex? A Response to Ann Fausto-
       Sterling', *Journal of Sex Research*, Vol. 39 (3), 2002, pp. 174–178.

49   Colin Pardoe, Ancillary Report on Individual x13001.

50   Maitland Gaol Admission Books, 1860, NRS 2317, NSW
       State Records.

51   Colin Pardoe, Ancillary Report on Individual x13001.

Chapter 2

1   The description of Jim Crow's execution derives from two
       newspaper articles: *The Maitland Mercury & Hunter River General
       Advertiser*, 28 April 1860, p. 2; *Empire*, 30 April 1860, p. 8.

2   *Maitland Mercury*, 28 April 1860.

3   *Empire*, 30 April 1860.

4   Jim Crow's death certificate states that he was 25 when hanged
       in 1860. By contrast, his prison admission record (Maitland
       Gaol Admission Books, 1860, NRS 2317, NSW State Records)
       states his birth year as 1837.

5   Peter Cunningham, *Two Years in New South Wales*, Henry
       Colburn, London, 1827, p. 147, in Helen Brayshaw, *Aborigines
       of the Hunter Valley*, Scone, 1987, p. 23.

6   Reg Ford, *Clarence Town: Erring-I to River Port*, Clarence
       Town, 1987, p. 7.

7   Mark Staniforth, 'Deptford Shipyard', website of the
       Australian Historic Shipwreck Preservation Project, www.
       ahspp.org.au/wp-content/uploads/Deptford.pdf. Accessed 23
       August 2013.

8   Ford, p. 4. Ford does not cite sources for this translation.
       Erring-I or Erringhi is a name popularly used in the town.

9   Henry Reynolds, *With the White People*, Penguin, Ringwood,
       1990, p. 132.

10   Brayshaw, p. 36.

11   Alfred Howitt, *Native Tribes of South-East Australia*, The Macmillan Company, New York, 1904, p. 574.

12   See the map in Jim Wafer and Amanda Lissarague, *A Handbook of Aboriginal Languages*, Nambucca Heads, 2008, p. 161.

13   Texts that point towards the Gringai being a sub-group of the Worimi include: Walter John Enright, 'Further Notes on the Worimi', *Mankind*, Vol. 1 (7), 1933, p. 161; Norman Tindale, *Aboriginal Tribes of Australia*, Berkeley, 1974, in Wafer and Lissarague, p. 188; John Ramsland, *The Rainbow Beach Man: The Life and Times of Les Ridgeway Worimi Elder*, Melbourne, 2009, p. 44. Those that argue the other case include James Miller, *Koori: A Will to Win*, Sydney, 1985, p. xv.

14   George MacKenzie to Colonial Secretary, 1833, Doc 102/103, Special Bundle 4/6666B.3, NSW State Records.

15   Brayshaw, p. 36.

16   The blanket returns for localities in the Hunter Valley and Williams River Valley are contained in Special Bundles 4/6666B.3 and 4/1133.3, NSW State Records.

17   For example, traditional names are absent for many of the women listed in Dungog in 1837 and 1838, and women are not listed at all in 1842.

18   Although the registers of 1837 and 1838 do individually list four boys aged between 10 and 13.

19   All contained within Special Bundle 4/1133.3.

20   Note, Doc 5, Special Bundle 4/1133.3, NSW State Records.

21   I thank Antoinette Smith and Lindy Allen for explaining this complexity to me.

22   Dungog blanket return, 1837, Special Bundle 4/1133.3.

23   Boatfall Creek, Record ID: NSW5331, Gazetteer of Australian Place Names, Geoscience Australia website: http://www.ga/gov.au/place-name. Accessed 19 May 2014.

24   Dungog blanket returns, 1837. Both 'Boat Fall' and 'Boatfall' are used in the lists.

25   Dungog blanket returns, 1837 and 1838; Canningalla Station was the home of the Dowlings, an influential settler family.

26   Although these men may have also been misclassified in 1837 through clerical error.

27   Ford, pp. 25, 27, 39.

28   'Report from the Select Committee on the Condition of the
      Aborigines', 1845, Replies of Dungog Bench, p. 6, in Michael
      Williams, 'Aboriginal people – the Gringai', History in the
      Williams River Valley website, http://williamsvalleyhistory.
      org/aborigines-gringai/. Accessed 15 October 2013.

29   Ibid.

30   Dungog Blanket Returns, 1838 and 1842.

31   Brayshaw, p. 22.

32   Reynolds, 1990, pp. 88 and 91.

33   Heather Goodall, 'New South Wales', in Ann McGrath (ed.),
      Contested Ground: Australian Aborigines Under the British Crown,
      Sydney, 1995, p. 68.

34   Henry Reynolds, 'Aborigines and European Social Hierarchy',
      Aboriginal History, Vol. 7, 1983, pp. 124–133.

35   *Maitland Mercury*, 15 March 1860, p. 1.

36   Goodall, p. 70.

37   Maitland Gaol Admission Books, 1860.

38   *Maitland Mercury*, 19 June 1860, p. 3.

39   Ford, p. 27

40   Colin Pardoe, Ancillary Report on Individual x13001.

41   Regina v Jim Crow, Maitland Circuit Court Depositions, 1860,
      9/6432, NRS 880, NSW State Records.

42   Henry Reynolds, *Frontier*, Allen & Unwin, North Sydney,
      1987, *passim*; Reynolds, 1990, p. 214.

43   Reynolds, 1987, p. 58.

44   Bain Attwood, *The Making of the Aborigines*, Allen & Unwin,
      Sydney, 1989, p. 106, citing: Bessie Harrison, 'The Making of a
      Town', Royal Historical Society of Victoria, MS 4814; and John
      H Leslie and Helen C Cowie (eds), *The Wind Still Blows*, Sale,
      1973, pp. 28–29.

45   R v Jim Crow, Depositions.

46   Ibid.

47   Amanda Kaladelfos, 'The Politics of Punishment: Rape and
      the Death Penalty in Colonial Australia, 1841–1901', *History
      Australia*, Vol. 9 (1), 2012, p. 165.

48 *Hurled Into Eternity: The 16 Executions at Maitland Gaol*, Maitland City Council, Maitland, 2012.

49 Ibid., p. 155.

50 The depositions for the second case were taken in September 1860, but the trial took place in 1861.

51 Regina v John Laver and Regina v Jeremiah Driscoll, both within Maitland Circuit Court Depositions, 1860.

52 *Sydney Morning Herald*, 13 September 1860, p. 4.

53 Maitland Gaol Admission Books, 1860.

54 *Sydney Morning Herald*, 18 March 1861, p. 3.

55 *Maitland Mercury & Hunter River General Advertiser*, 13 March 1860, p. 1.

56 Regina v Billy and Tommy, Maitland Circuit Court Depositions, 1860, 9/6432, NRS 880, NSW State Records.

57 *Maitland Mercury*, 13 March 1860, p. 4.

58 Gail S Goodman, 'Children's Testimony in Historical Perspective', *Journal of Social Issues*, Vol 40(2), 1984, p. 13.

59 R v Billy and Tommy, Depositions.

60 R v Laver and R v Billy and Tommy, Depositions.

61 *The Maitland Mercury*, 15 March 1860, p. 1.

62 Kristyn Harman, 'The Same Measure of Justice: Aboriginal Convicts in the Australian Penal Colonies', *Australian Studies*, Vol. 1, 2009, p. 10.

63 *Maitland Mercury*, 15 March 1860, p. 1.

64 R v Jim Crow, Depositions.

65 *Maitland Mercury*, 22 March 1860, p. 2.

66 Eades cites Kenneth Liberman, who terms this phenomenon 'gratuitous concurrence'. K Liberman, *Understanding interaction in Central Australia: an ethnomethodological study of Australian Aboriginal People*, Routledge & Kegan Paul, Boston, in Diane Eades, *Aboriginal Ways of Using English*, Aboriginal Studies Press, Canberra, 2013, pp. 100–101.

67 Eades, p. 101.

68 Regina v Thomas Duffy and John McMillan, Maitland Circuit Court Depositions, 1860.

69 Regina v Beamish, Maitland Circuit Court Depositions, 1860.

70   Harman, p. 10.

71   Bevan Report (1913), 3 December, CRS A3, NT 1914/426, National Archives of Australia, in Mark Finnane and Heather Douglas, *Indigenous Crime and Settler Law*, Palgrave Macmillan, Houndmills, 2012, p. 75.

72   'Windeyer, Sir William Charles (1834–1897), Australian Dictionary of Biography, National Centre of Biography, ANU, http://adb.anu.edu/biography/windeyer-sir-william-charles-1062/text8145. Accessed 13 March 2013.

73   *The Maitland Mercury*, 15 March 1860, p. 1.

74   Ibid.

75   R v Jim Crow, Depositions; *Maitland Mercury*, 15 March 1860, p. 1.

76   *Maitland Mercury*, 15 March 1860, p. 1.

77   Attwood, 1989, pp. 126–127.

78   R v Jim Crow, Depositions.

79   *Maitland Mercury*, 15 March 1860, p. 1.

80   Kaladelfos, p. 157.

81   Mark Finnane and Jonathan Richards, 'Aboriginal Violence and State Response: Histories, Policies, Legacies in Queensland 1860–1940', *Australian and New Zealand Journal of Criminology*, Vol. 43 (2), 2010, p. 252, in Kaladelfos, p. 168.

82   *Maitland Mercury*, 13 September 1848, p. 2, in Kristyn Harman, *Aboriginal Convicts*, University of New South Wales Press, Sydney, 2012, p. 139.

83   Ibid.

84   Martha Rutledge, 'Stephen, Sir Alfred (1802–1894)', Australian Dictionary of Biography, National Centre of Biography, Australian National University, http://adb.anu.edu.au/biography/stephen-sir-alfred-1291/text7645. Accessed 15 September 2013.

Chapter 3

1   *Empire*, 30 July 1860, p. 5.

2   Ibid.; *Sydney Morning Herald*, 14 August 1860, p. 3.

3   *The Maitland Mercury & Hunter River General Advertiser*, 15 March 1860, p. 1.

4   *Empire*, 30 July 1860, p. 5; *Sydney Morning Herald*, 14 August 1860, p. 3.

5   Ibid.

6   *Empire*, 30 July 1860, p. 5.

7   Ibid.

8   Ibid.

9   *Empire*, 30 July 1860, p. 5; *Sydney Morning Herald*, 14 August 1860, p. 3.

10   Ibid.

11   Ibid.

12   *Freeman's Journal*, 8 August 1860, p. 3; *Bendigo Advertiser*, 18 August 1860, p. 3.

13   *Empire*, 30 July 1860, p. 5.

14   Pickering, Michael, 'Where are the Stories?', *The Public Historian*, Vol. 32 (1), 2010, pp. 82–84. For more about the role of amateur collectors, see Tom Griffiths, *Hunters and Collectors*, Oakleigh, 1996. For a discussion of the role of paid collectors, see Paul Turnbull's 'The Body and Soul Snatchers', *Eureka Street*, Vol. 7 (7), September 1997, pp. 34–38.

15   Bronwen Douglas and Chris Ballard (eds), *Foreign Bodies: Oceania and the Science of Race 1750–1940*, ANU Press, Canberra, 2008, p. xii.

16   Douglas identifies the Linnaen system of classification as a turning point in the development of a biological idea of race. See: Douglas, 'Climate to Crania: Science and the Racialization of Human Difference', in Douglas & Ballard.

17   Paul Turnbull, 'Phrenologists and the Construction of the Aboriginal Race, c.1790–1830', *History Compass*, Vol. 5 (1), 2007, p. 27.

18   Helen MacDonald, *Human Remains: Episodes in Human Dissection*, Carlton, 2005, p. 104.

19   Douglas, p. 53.

20   Paul Turnbull, 'British Anthropological Thought in Colonial Practice', in Douglas and Ballard (eds), p. 207; Cressida Fforde,

Collecting the Dead: Archaeology and the Reburial Issue, London, 2004, p. 20.

21 MacDonald, 2005, p. 108; Turnbull, 2008, p. 213.

22 Fforde 2004, pp. 27–29.

23 Ibid., p. 28.

24 Michael Bulmer, *Francis Galton: Pioneer of Heredity and Biometry*, The Johns Hopkins University Press, Baltimore, 2003, p. 32.

25 Helen MacDonald, *Possessing the Dead*, Melbourne University Press, Carlton, 2010.

26 Paul Turnbull, 'Scientific Theft of Remains in Colonial Australia', *Australian Indigenous Law Review*, Vol. 11 (1), 2007, pp. 97–98.

27 Roger Cooter, *The Cultural Meaning of Popular Science: Phrenology and the Organization of Consent in Nineteenth-century Britain*, Cambridge University Press, New York, p. 3.

28 Ibid., p. 522; AS Hamilton, *Practical Phrenology: A Lecture on the Heads, Casts of the Heads, and Characters of the Maungatapu Murderers*, Nelson, 1866.

29 Spurzheim added three organs to Combe's system – Conscientiousness, Time and Order – and George Combe contributed Concentrativeness. Cooter, p. 116.

30 Roger Cooter, pp. 89, 283, 296; John van Wyhe, *Phrenology and the Origins of Victorian Scientific Naturalism*, Ashgate, Aldershot, 2004, pp. 27–28.

31 John van Wyhe, 'The Diffusion of Phrenology', in *Science in the Marketplace*, Aileen Fyfe and Bernard Lightman (eds), University of Chicago Press, 2007, p. 82.

32 Cooter, p, 120.

33 Cooter, p. 117.

34 Ibid, p. 83.

35 Cooter, p. 21.

36 David de Giustino, *Conquest of Mind: Phrenology and Victorian Social Thought*, Croom Helm, London, 1975, p. 136. Orson Squire Fowler, part of the influential Fowler family that made phrenology a household practice in the US, published a pamphlet called *Temperance, Founded on Phrenology and Physiology*, which

ran to more than 20 editions. The 24th edition, published in 1846, can be viewed as a free Google Book online.

37   David de Giustino, 1975, p. 119.

38   *The Brisbane Courier*, 6 August 1896, p. 6; *The Northern Miner*, 25 July 1893, p. 3.

39   Fforde p. 23; A rationale for establishing the National Museum of Victoria was to prevent the 'dissipation' of working classes (David Goodman, 'Fear of Circuses: Founding the National Museum of Victoria', *Continuum*, Vol. 3 (1), 1990, p. 21.)

40   George Nadel, *Australia's Colonial Culture*, FW Cheshire, Melbourne, 1957, pp. 139–142.

41   David de Giustino, p. 145; Cooter, p. 32.

42   Henry Lawson, *While the Billy Boils* (ebook), University of Adelaide. Available online: http://ebooks.adelaide.edu.au/l/lawson/henry/while_the_billy_boils/complete.html. Accessed 19 May 2014.

43   Ibid.

44   'Tasma' (Jessie Couvreur), 'What an artist discovered in Tasmania', in *A Sydney Sovereign: Tasma* (Introduced and Edited by Michael Ackland), Angus & Robertson, Pymble, 1993, p. 15. The story was published in Garnet Walch (ed), *Australasia: An Intercolonial Christmas Annual*, George Robertson, Melbourne, 1878.

45   Wilson, Janice Evelyn, 'Signs of the Mind: Science, Psychological Knowledge and Social Hegemony in Colonial Australia', PhD Thesis, University of Western Australia, 1994, Microfiche mc G 6631, National Library of Australia.

46   Australian scholarship that touches on phrenology's impact in Australia includes: Jill Dimond, 'Ned Kelly's Skull', Issue 211, *Overland*, 2013; David de Giustino, 'Reforming the commonwealth of Thieves: British Phrenologists and Australia', *Victorian Studies*, Vol. 15 (4), 1972, pp. 439–461; Paul Turnbull, 'British Anatomists, Phrenologists and the Construction of the Aboriginal race, c. 1790–1830', *History Compass*, Vol. 5(1), 2007, pp. 26–50; Paul Turnbull, 'Rare work amongst the professors', in Barbara Creed and Jeanette Hoorn (eds), *Body Trade: Captivity, Cannibalism and Colonialism in the Pacific*, pp. 3–23; Dean Wilson, 'Explaining the 'Criminal' Ned Kelly's Death Mask', *The La Trobe Journal*,

No 69, 2002, pp. 51–58. Phrenology is also discussed as a dominant idea in Australian culture within broader works. For example, Michael Roe, *Quest for Authority in Eastern Australia 1835–1851*, Halstead Press, Kingsgrove, 1965, pp. 161–164, and Nadel, pp. 139–142.

47   M. John Thearle, 'The Rise and Fall of Phrenology in Australia', *Australian and New Zealand Journal of Psychiatry*, Vol. 27, 1993, pp. 518-525.

48   *The Brisbane Courier*, 1 August 1877, p. 1.

49   *South Australian Chronicle and Weekly Mail*, 13 November 1880, p. 26.

50   *South Australian Register*, 31 July 1890, p. 3. The contemporary term for this group is 'Bushmen'.

51   In an 1819 census known as 'The Landsborough List', a Hamilton family is listed that includes a child called Archibald (http://www.ayrshireroots.com/Genealogy/Records/Census/1820s/Landsborough/November%201819%20G-H.htm). The names of the parents – Agnes Sillars and Edward Hamilton – match those on Hamilton's death certificate, and the age of his death in 1884 – 65 – correlates with this date.

52   Marriage certificate of Emma Elizabeth Joscelyne and Archibald Hamilton, Tasmanian Archive and Heritage Office, SC89/1/2 1871, Documents in cases of divorce – Hamilton v Hamilton.

53   Papers of Agnes Hamilton-Grey, 'A Few Reminiscences', Bundle (ii)(c), Box 1, ML MSS 294, Mitchell Library, State Library of New South Wales.

54   Cooter, p. 157, p. 284. Cooter drew the quote about the "dirty old wench" from Elizabeth Eastlake, Journals and Correspondence, 1895, I, pp. 65–66.

55   *The Falkirk Herald*, 20 October 1859, p. 3.

56   *Newcastle Courant*, 11 June 1841, p. 3.

57   *South Australian Register*, 27 September 1871, p. 7.

58   *The Courier* (Hobart), 6 December 1854, p. 3.

59   AS Hamilton, Character sketch of Robert Walker, Tasmania June 1855, University of Tasmania Library Special and Rare Materials Collection, Australia, http://eprints.utas.edu.au/6199/. Accessed 22 June 2013.

60 AS Hamilton, 'Full Study of Character of Wilson Esq. (Alfred Deakin)', Alfred Deakin Papers, Reel 28079, National Library of Australia.

61 R Norris, 'Deakin, Alfred (1856–1919)', Australian Dictionary of Biography, Volume 8, MUP, 1981. Available online: http://adb.anu.edu.au/biography/deakin-alfred-5927/text10099. Accessed 11 July 2014.

62 *Wagga Wagga Advertiser,* 9 November 1880, p. 4.

63 Hamilton Divorce File. For the biography of Archibald McDonald, see Design & Art Australia Online, an online database for researchers in art and design, www.daao.org/bio/archibald-mcdonald/biography/ (Accessed 14 May 2014). I was made aware of this photograph through Jill Dimond's article, 'Ned Kelly's Skull', which appeared in the winter edition of *Overland* magazine in 2013.

64 In *The Argus* of 9 March 1871 (p.5), Hamilton is described as a potential candidate in the elections for Geelong West.

65 'A few reminiscences', Agnes Hamilton-Grey Papers, Bundle (ii)(c), Box 1, ML MSS 294, Mitchell Library, State Library of New South Wales, p. 9.

66 De Giustino, 1975, p. 223.

67 Archibald Sillars Hamilton, Death Certificate, NSW Registry of Births, Deaths and Marriages, No 1884/005206.

68 Turnbull, 2007, p. 34.

69 George Combe, *The Constitution of Man*, Edinburgh, 1828, p. 164, in Henry Reynolds, 'Racial Thought in Early Colonial Australia', *Australian Journal of Politics and History*, Vol. 20, 1974, pp. 45–53.

70 'Report of the Select Committee of the Legislative Council on Aborigines', Melbourne, 1858, pp. 46–47.

71 Hamilton Collection, Accession number x12962.

72 Ibid., x12922.

73 Ibid, x 12997A.

74 Wilson, p. 53.

75 Hamilton Collection, Melbourne Museum, Accession number x72603. Bagdad is a small town north of Hobart.

76 *The Dundee Advertiser,* 28 August 1866, p. 4.

77 Hamilton Collection, Melbourne Museum.

78 These three Tasmanians are John Drake (X72602), Charles Marshall (X72603) and Thomas Wilkinson (X72621). The information about St Mary's Hospital, Hobart, was published on the website of the University of Tasmania Archives. Available online: http://www.utas.edu.au/__data/assets/pdf_file/0004/64246/rs_28-St-Marys-Hospital-Hobart-1841-1862.pdf. Accessed 3 March 2014.

79 Jill Dimond, 'Ned Kelly's Skull', *Overland*, Issue 211, Winter, 2013.

80 Natalie Muller, 'DNA confirms Ned Kelly's remains', *Australian Geographic*, 1 September 2011. Available at: http://www.australiangeographic.com.au/news/2011/09/dna-confirms-ned-kellys-remains. Accessed 16 May 2014.

81 Dimond, 2013.

82 Ibid., X72606 and X81479

83 *Moreton Bay Courier*, 7 August 1860, p. 4; *Sydney Morning Herald*, 1 August 1860, p. 8; *Bendigo Advertiser*, 18 August 1860, p. 3; *Launceston Examiner*, 1 September 1860, p. 2.

84 *Sydney Morning Herald*, 14 August 1860, p. 3. All information about Hamilton's 1860 trial derives from this newspaper article.

85 For example, the article about the committal proceeding in *Empire* refers to dates that do not match up with the days of the week for the 1860 calendar.

86 See Hamilton's two pamphlets: 'Abstract of a lecture on Criminal Legislation, Prison Discipline and the Causes of Crime, and on Capital Punishment', Sydney, 1863; and 'Practical Phrenology: A Lecture on the heads, casts of the heads, and characters of the Maungatapu Murderers, Levy, Kelly, Sullivan, and Burgess', Nelson, 1866.

87 Helen MacDonald describes the spectre of Burke and Hare as a "useful myth" that legitimised the removal of bodies from poor houses and hospitals before relatives could claim them (2010, p. 223).

88 *The Courier*, 30 April 1862, p. 2.

89 South Australian Register, 12 July 1865, p. 2.

90 Empire, 9 November, 1866, p. 3.

91 Sydney Morning Herald, 22 April 1871, p. 9; Australian Town and Country Journal, 29 April 1871, p. 11.

92 Australian Town and Country Journal, 29 April 1871, p. 5.

93 An 1835 baptismal certificate for a girl of this name from Sudbury, Suffolk, indicates that she was probably 18 when they married. Marriage certificate of Emma Elizabeth Joscelyne and Archibald Hamilton; Baptismal Record for Emma Elizabeth Joscelyne (19 April 1835), Non-Conformist and Non-Parochial Registers for England & Wales, 1835, p. 95, RG4/1861, Records of the General Register Office, Government Social Survey Department, and Office of Population Censuses and Surveys, Registrar General, National Archives, Kew. Accessed through Ancestry.com.

94 Marriage certificate of Archibald Sillars Hamilton and Emily Ellis, No 4109, Victorian Registry of Births, Deaths and Marriages.

95 Jill Dimond, 'From the Lips of a Lady', *Australian Literary Studies*, Vol. 21 (3), 2004, p. 338.

96 Hamilton Divorce File.

97 Petition of Emma Elizabeth Hamilton. Hamilton v Hamilton divorce file.

98 Penny Russell, *A Wish of Distinction*, Melbourne University Press, Carlton, 1994, p. 166.

99 Ginger Frost, 'Bigamy and Cohabitation in Victorian England', *Journal of Family History*, Vol. 22, 1997, p. 290.

100 Letter from AS Hamilton to Emma Elizabeth Hamilton, Hamilton divorce file.

101 *Empire*, 18 June 1863, p. 8; *Maitland Mercury* 4 August 1874, p. 1.

102 *Empire*, 9 November, 1866, p. 3.

103 Papers of Agnes Hamilton-Grey, 'A Few Reminiscences', Bundle (ii)(c), Box 1, ML MSS 294, Mitchell Library, State Library of New South Wales, p. 9.

104 X72598, Hamilton Collection.

105 *The Courier* (Hobart), 6 December 1854, p. 3; *The Colonial Times*, 7 December 1854, p. 2.

106 *The Courier* (Brisbane), 23 April 1862, p. 2; *South Australian Register*, 2 May 1865, p. 2; *The Maitland Mercury*, 8 September 1860, p. 3.

107 *The Maitland Mercury*, 15 March 1860, p. 1

108 *The Dundee Advertiser*, 28 August 1866, p. 4.

109 Agnes Hamilton-Grey, 'A Few Reminiscences', p. 9.

110 Ibid.

111 *The Maitland Mercury*, 20 September 1869, p. 3; Ibid., 15 March 1860, p. 1; *The Courier* (Brisbane), 30 May 1862, p. 1.

112 *The Courier* (Hobart), 7 May 1855, p. 3. Today's value calculated using the real price index, www.measuringworth.com. Accessed 30 May 2013.

113 *The Maitland Mercury*, 8 August 1861, p. 3; *Empire*, 18 June 1863, p. 8.

114 CN Connolly, 'Miners' Rights', in Ann Curthoys and Andrew Markus (eds), *Who Are Your Enemies: Racism and the Australian Working Class*, Hale and Iremonger, Neutral Bay, 1978.

115 *The Maitland Mercury*, 8 August 1861, p. 3.

116 *Empire*, 18 June 1863, p. 8.

117 Hamilton, 1863.

118 *The Courier* (Brisbane), 10 June 1862, p. 2.

119 Hamilton, 1866, p. 3.

120 Hamilton, 1863, p. 11.

121 *The Maitland Mercury*, 9 June 1860, p. 2.

122 *Wellington Independent*, 4 September 1866, p. 6.

123 Ibid.

124 Ibid.

125 John van Wyhe, 'Was phrenology a reform science? Towards a new generalization for phrenology', *History of Science*, Vol. xlii, 2004, p. 322.

126 Letters from Spurzheim to Honorine Pothier, 20 September 1814 and 1 September 1814, Johann Gaspar Spurzheim papers (B MS c 22), Boston Medical Library in the Countway Library of Medicine, in John van Wyhe, *Phrenology and the Origins of Victorian Scientific Naturalism*, Ashgate, 2004, p. 32.

127 Van Wyhe, 'Was phrenology a reform science?', p. 322.

128 *Empire*, 2 July 1873, p. 2.

Chapter 4

1   *Sydney Morning Herald*, 13 March 1889, pp. 2, 5 and 11. In later life, Hamilton's third wife went by the name Agnes Hamilton-Grey. However, for simplicity, I have chosen to refer to her in this chapter as Agnes Hamilton (or simply Agnes), as this was how she signed her correspondence in relation to the transfer of the Hamilton collection. Where I refer simply to 'Hamilton', I mean AS Hamilton.

2   "The non-fulfillment of her histrionic gifts" would become a major theme of Agnes Hamilton's reminiscences and biography, penned in third-person during the 1920s. Hamilton-Grey Papers, ML MSS 294, Mitchell Library, State Library of New South Wales.

3   The advertisement, published in the *Sydney Morning Herald* on 22 July 1884, p. 10, states: "Mrs A. Sellars [sic] Hamilton, only pupil (eight years) of the late A.S. Hamilton, Phrenologist, will practise her profession. 27 Hunter Street, two doors from Pitt Street."

4   The first two suggestions were made by James Smith of *The Argus*, in his letter of 8 Jan 1885, and the third by Louisa Dutrue, Agnes Hamilton-Grey Correspondence, Box 1, ML MSS 294, Mitchell Library, State Library of New South Wales.

5   Jill Dimond, 'From the Lips of a Lady', *Australian Literary Studies*, Vol. 21 (3), 2004, p. 344.

6   Letter from Mrs AM Hamilton to the Board of Trustees, 13 March 1889, Letter 333 of 1889, Box 142, VPRS805, Public Records Office of Victoria.

7   Letter from Mrs AM Hamilton to the Board of Trustees, 26 March 1889, Letter 393 of 1889, Box 142, VPRS805, Public Records Office of Victoria.

8   This is skull X72606, identified by the label as being that of a "highly cultivated medical man".

9   The crania marked as Tasmanian or New Zealander have all been repatriated.

10   Letter from Mrs AM Hamilton to the Board of Trustees, 2 April 1889, Letter 418 of 1889, Box 142, VPRS805, Public Records Office of Victoria.

11   Ibid.

12   Ibid.

13   Wreck Report for the 'Konoowarra', No. 3813, Brisbane
      Marine Board Office, 26 April 1889, Board of Trade. Available
      at: http://www.plimsoll.org/resources/SCCLibraries/
      WreckReports/15667.asp. Accessed 21 May 2014.

14   Letter from Mrs AM Hamilton to the Board of Trustees, 2
      April 1889.

15   *Bendigo Advertiser*, 26 April 1882, p. 2.

16   Last will and testament of Agnes Hamilton-Grey, Box 1,
      ML MSS 294, Mitchell Library, State Library of New South
      Wales.

17   Dimond, 2004, p. 344. Dimond bases this claim on
      correspondence provided to her by a family member of Agnes
      Hamilton.

18   Winston Gregory McMinn, *George Reid*, Melbourne
      University Press, 1989, p. 5.

19   Mary Morris from Museum Victoria alerted me to this
      possibility.

20   There are notes throughout the manuscripts that address the
      Mitchell Library staff. For example, her press clippings are
      accompanied by a shaky note: "Dear Sir, I have not the strength
      to put these in order. I have waited for it, thinking of a flush
      of energy – but it does not come. Pray excuse, AM Hamilton-
      Grey." Bundle (ii)(d), Box 1, Hamilton-Grey papers.

21   Letter from Mrs AM Hamilton to the Board of Trustees,
      13 March 1889.

22   Letter from Mrs AM Hamilton to the Board of Trustees, 1
      April 1889.

23   The Melbourne Intercolonial Exhibition of 1866–1867,
      the Melbourne International Exhibition of 1880, and the
      Melbourne Centennial International Exhibition of 1888.

24   Report of the Trustees of the Public Library, Museums, and
      National Gallery of Victoria, for 1889, p. 14.

25   The telegraphy courses ran until 1877. See: Carolyn Rasmussen,
      'Valuable, Practical Information', in Carolyn Rasmussen (ed),
      A Museum for the People, Scribe Publications, 2001, p. 86.

26   Ian Wilkinson, 'The Battle for the Museum: Frederick McCoy
      and the Establishment of the National Museum of Victoria at

the University of Melbourne', *Historical Records of Australian Science*, Vol. 11 (1), 1996, p. 1.

27 Ross Jones, *Humanity's Mirror*, Haddington Press, South Yarra, 2007, p. 5.

28 Report of the Trustees for 1875, p. 36; David Blair, 'Extinction of Aboriginal Tribes', *The Argus*, 5 December 1868; *Speculum*, No. 23, Feb 1891, in Ross Jones, 'Cadavers and the Social Dimension of Dissection', in Sarah Ferber and Sally Wilde (eds), *The Body Divided: Human Beings and Human 'Material' in Modern Medical History*, Ashgate, Farnham, 2011, p. 39.

29 Report of the Trustees for 1875, p. 36. Gareth Knapman, 'Resisting Man's Place in Nature: Frederick McCoy's decision to exclude humans from the National Museum of Victoria', Unpublished report, Department of Humanities, Melbourne Museum. A version of this paper is due for publication in the *Historical Records of Australian Science*, 2015.

30 Ibid, citing several letters from the Museum Victoria letter book: F. McCoy to R. Allin, 26 February 1868; F. McCoy to F. Tate, 15 April 1874; F. McCoy to J. Blackman, 25 May 1876, 199; F. McCoy to Mrs Turner, 3 September 1874; F. McCoy to J. Jenson, 3 September 1880; F. McCoy to Public Library, 30 May 1884.

31 Report of the Trustees for 1874–1875, p. 35.

32 Report of the Trustees for 1886, p. 27.

33 For example, during 1874–1875, a "native axe found near Hexham" was donated to the collection. See: Report of the Trustees for 1874–1875, p. 28.

34 Report of the Trustees for 1886, p. 20.

35 The documentation related to the two museums is variously held in the State Library of Victoria, the Victorian Public Record Office and archives of Museum Victoria.

36 Index to Inward Registered Correspondence, 1889–1892, Trustees of the Public Library, Museums and National Gallery of Victoria VPRS 801, Victorian Public Records Office.

37 Cover sheet, Letter from Mrs AM Hamilton to Board of Trustees, 13 March 1889.

38 Report of the Trustees for 1878, p. 37.

39   Letter from J Bevan to Board of Trustees regarding New Guinea Collection for sale, 14 Dec 1886, letter 597 of 1886, Box 128A, VPRS 805, Public Records Office of Victoria.

40   Register of the ethnographic collection, Department of Humanities, Melbourne Museum.

41   OR Rule Correspondence file, Correspondence of the Industrial and Technological Museum, Box 568, Museum Victoria Archives.

42   Minute Books of the Trustees of the Public Library, Gallery and Museums, Nov 1884–Oct 1890, MSF Vol. 2, State Library of Victoria; Minute Books of the Industrial and Technological Museum, Minute Book 2 (31 Jan 1888–16 Dec 1927), Melbourne Museum Archives.

43   See: Report of the Trustees for 1889.

44   Wagga Wagga Advertiser, 9 November 1889, p. 4. Newspaper reports from the days following the execution discuss how an 'exhibition' of the Kelly family at Apollo Hall was stopped. See *South Australian Advertiser*, 15 November 1880, p. 5; *Goulburn Herald and Chronicle*, 17 November 1880, p. 4. Jill Dimond (2014) cites a report in the Brisbane *Courier*, 20 November 1880, p. 5.

45   *The Queenslander*, 6 November 1880, p. 1.

46   Letter from the Board of Trustees, 1880, Page 97, Outward Letter Book, National Museum 1870–1885, VPRS5833, Public Record Office of Victoria.

47   RTM Pescott, *Collections of a Century*, National Museum of Victoria, Melbourne, p. 94.

48   Ross Jones, *Humanity's Mirror*, pp. 110–130; KF Russell, 'Richard James Arthur Berry', Australian Dictionary of Biography, Volume 7, MUP, 1979. Available at http://adb.anu.edu.au/biography/berry-richard-james-arthur-5220. Accessed 24 April 2014.

49   Richard Berry, 'Chance and Circumstance', Typescript memoirs, Papers of Leonard JT Murphy, UMA 91/114, University of Melbourne Archives, pp. 3–10.

50   Ibid, p. 188; p. 127.

51   Ibid, p. 127.

52   William Crowther, Medical Journal of Australia, 2 February 1934, p. 147, in Mary Cawte, 'Craniometry and Eugenics in

Australia: R. J. A Berry and the quest for social efficiency',
Historical Studies, Vol. 22 (86), 1986, pp. 43–44.

53 Richard Berry and AWD Robertson, 'Dioptrographic Tracings
in Four Normae of Fifty-Two Tasmanian Crania', *Transactions
of the Royal Society of Victoria*, Vol. 5, 1909.

54 CO Whitman (ed.), 'Microscopy', *The American Naturalist*, Vol.
20 (4), 1886, pp. 406–407.

55 *The British Medical Journal*, Vol. 2 (2551), 1909, p. 1490.

56 On page 3 of 'Dioptrographic Tracings in Three Normae of
Ninety Australian Aboriginal Crania', Transactions of the
Royal Society of Victoria, Vol. 6, 1914, Berry and Robertson
quote one critic who said that "the scientific value of the
publication would have been greatly advanced if the authors
had included the results of the elaborate study they have made
of this new collection of Tasmanian crania".

57 HB Allen, University of Melbourne, Medical School Jubilee
1914, Carlton, 1914, p. 53, in Ross Jones, 'Cadavers and the
Social Dimension of Dissection', p. 40.

58 Richard Berry and AWD Robertson, 1914, p. 5.

59 Ibid.

60 The mystery of these strange holes was solved by Dr Soren
Blau of the Victorian Institute of Forensic Medicine and her
colleagues in the UK, for whose expertise I am extremely
grateful. Historian of medicine John Kirkup describes
trepanation equipment from this period in *The Evolution of
Surgical Instruments: An Illustrated History from Ancient Times
to the Twentieth Century*, Norman Publishing, Novato, 2006,
pp. 295–297.

61 Danielle S Kurin discusses the post-procedure survival rates of
individuals trepanned in prehistoric Peru, and how this can be
assessed, in 'Trepanation in South-Central Peru During the
Early Late Intermediate Period (ca. AD 1000–1250)', *American
Journal of Physical Anthropology*, Vol. 152 (4), 2013, p. 486.

62 The skull of Drake is X72602, and 'No.19' is X72605.

63 For example, three individuals within the collection are
labelled as coming from Jones Creek, but which Jones Creek
this might be is difficult to ascertain.

64 Agnes Hamilton-Grey, Draft of 'How I at last came to write
about Henry Kendall, commencing with "Our Son of the

Woods, Henry Kendall and his poetry", Agnes Hamilton-Grey Papers, Bundle (vi)(a), Box 2, ML MSS 294, Mitchell Library, State Library of New South Wales, p. 1.

Afterword: Jim Crow Found

1 John Danalis, *Riding the Black Cockatoo* (ebook), Allen & Unwin, 2009, pp. 45–47.

2 James Waddell, *A History of St Peter's Church, East Maitland, NSW*, Maitland, 1996, p. 26.

Bibliography

Primary Sources

Museum Victoria

Hamilton Collection, Restricted Collections, Humanities Department, Melbourne Museum, and accompanying files, particularly the Jim Crow File.

Pardoe, Colin. 'Ancillary Report on Individual x13001', Jim Crow File, Restricted Collections, Humanities Department, Melbourne Museum, 2013.

Register of the Ethnographic Collection, Department of Humanities, Melbourne Museum.

Oliver Rule file, Correspondence of the Industrial and Technological Museum, Box 568, Museum Victoria Archives.

Manuscripts and pamphlets

Berry, Richard, 'Chance and Circumstance', Typescript memoirs, Papers of Leonard JT Murphy, UMA 91/114, University of Melbourne Archives.

Agnes Hamilton-Grey Papers, ML MSS 294, Mitchell Library, State Library of New South Wales.

Hamilton, AS, 'Full Study of Character of Wilson Esq. (Alfred Deakin)', Alfred Deakin Papers, Reel 28079, National Library of Australia

Hamilton, AS, Character sketch of Robert Walker, Tasmania, June 1855. University of Tasmania Library Special and Rare Materials Collection, Australia. Available online at http://eprints.utas.edu.au/6199/.

Hamilton, AS, Estimate of the Character of Walter Filmer, 1871, Newcastle Cultural Collections. Available online at http://collections.ncc.nsw.gov.au/keemu/pages/nrm/index.htm.

Hamilton, AS, 'Abstract of a lecture on Criminal Legislation, Prison Discipline and the Causes of Crime, and on Capital Punishment', Sydney, 1863.

Hamilton, AS, 'Practical Phrenology: A Lecture on the Heads, Casts of the Heads, and Characters of the Maungatapu Murderers', Nelson, 1866.

Government Archives

Archibald Sillars Hamilton, Death Certificate, NSW Registry of Births, Deaths and Marriages, No 1884/005206.

Archibald Sillars Hamilton and Emily Ellis, Marriage Certificate, Victorian Registry of Births, Deaths and Marriages, No 4109.

Hamilton Divorce File, Tasmanian Archive and Heritage Office, SC89/1/2 1871, Documents in cases of divorce – Hamilton v Hamilton.

Jim Crow, Death Certificate, NSW Registry of Births, Deaths and Marriages, No 1860/004431.

Maitland Circuit Court Depositions, 1860, 9/6432, NRS 880, NSW State Records.

Maitland Gaol Admission Books, 1860, NRS 2317, NSW State Records.

Report of the Select Committee of the Legislative Council on the Aborigines (Victoria), Melbourne, 1858–1859.

Special Bundle 4/1133.3 (1837–1844), NSW State Records.

Special Bundle 4/6666B.3 (1833–1835), NSW State Records.

Documents related to the Board of Trustees of the Public Library, Museums, and National Gallery of Victoria

Inward letter registers, VPRS 800 and 801, Public Record Office of Victoria.

Inward correspondence, VPRS 805, Public Record Office of Victoria.

Outward Letter Book, National Museum 1870–1885, VPRS5833, Public Record Office of Victoria.

Minute Books of the Trustees of the Public Library, Gallery and Museums, Nov 1884–Oct 1890, MSF Vol. 2, State Library of Victoria.

Reports of the Trustees of the Public Library, Museums, and National Gallery of Victoria for 1874–1875, 1878, 1886, 1889. These are available electronically through the Parliament of Victoria website, www.parliament.vic.gov.au/publications.

Minute Books of the Industrial and Technological Museum, Minute Book 2 (31 Jan 1888–16 Dec 1927), Melbourne Museum Archives.

Newspapers

Australian Town and Country Journal, 1871.
Bell's Life in Sydney and Sporting Reviewer, 1847.
Bendigo Advertiser, 1856, 1860, 1882.
The Canberra Times, 1960, 1963.
The Colonial Times, 1854.
The Courier (Brisbane), 1862, 1877, 1893.
The Courier (Hobart), 1846, 1854, 1855.
The Dundee Advertiser, 1866.
Empire, 1853, 1860, 1863, 1866, 1873.
Freeman's Journal, 1860.
Goulburn Herald and Chronicle, 1880.
Launceston Examiner, 1860.
Leeds Intelligencer, 1844.
Maitland Mercury & Hunter River General Advertiser, 1860, 1861, 1869, 1874.
Moreton Bay Courier, 1860.
The Argus, 1868, 1871.
The Newcastle Chronicle, 1871.
The Northern Miner, 1893.
The Queenslander, 1880.
Portland Guardian and Normanby General Advertiser, 1868.
South Australian Advertiser, 1880.
South Australian Register, 1865, 1871.
Sydney Morning Herald, 1860, 1861, 1871, 1884, 1889.
Wagga Wagga Advertiser, 1880.
Wellington Independent, 1866.

Scientific Publications

Richard Berry and AWD Robertson, 'Dioptrographic Tracings in Four Normae of Fifty-Two Tasmanian Crania', *Transactions of the Royal Society of Victoria*, Vol. 5, 1909.

Richard Berry and AWD Robertson, 'Dioptrographic Tracings in Three Normae of Ninety Australian Aboriginal Crania', *Transactions of the Royal Society of Victoria*, Vol. 6, 1914.

The British Medical Journal, Vol. 2 (2551), 1909, p. 1490.

Works of Fiction

Lawson, Henry, *While the Billy Boils* (ebook), University of Adelaide. Available online: http://ebooks.adelaide.edu.au/l/lawson/henry/while_the_billy_boils/complete.html.

'Tasma' (Jessie Couvreur), 'What an artist discovered in Tasmania', in A Sydney Sovereign: Tasma (Introduced and Edited by Michael Ackland), Angus & Robertson, Pymble, 1993.

Other

Konoowarra', No. 3813, Brisbane Marine Board Office, 26 April 1889, Board of Trade. Available at: http://www.plimsoll.org/resources/SCCLibraries/WreckReports/15667.asp. Accessed 21 May 2014.

Secondary Sources

Australian Dictionary of Biography, National Centre of Biography, Canberra, http://adb.anu.edu.au/biography.

Attwood, Bain, *Telling the Truth About Aboriginal History*, Allen & Unwin, Crows Nest, 2005.

Attwood, Bain, *The Making of the Aborigines*, Allen & Unwin, Sydney, 1989.

Brayshaw, Helen, *Aborigines of the Hunter Valley*, Scone & Upper Hunter Historical Society, Scone, 1987.

Broome, Richard, *Aboriginal Victorians*, Allen & Unwin, Sydney, 2005.

Brown, Peter, 'Sex determination of Aboriginal crania from the Murray River Valley', *Archaeology in Oceania*, Vol. 16 (1), 1981, pp. 53–63.

Bulmer, Michael, *Francis Galton: Pioneer of Heredity and Biometry*, The Johns Hopkins University Press, Baltimore, 2003.

Cawte, Mary, 'Craniometry and Eugenics in Australia: R. J. A Berry and the quest for social efficiency', *Historical Studies*, Vol. 22 (86), 1986, pp. 35–53.

Connolly, CN, 'Miners' Rights', in Ann Curthoys and Andrew Markus (eds), *Who Are Your Enemies: Racism and the Australian Working Class*, Hale and Iremonger, Neutral Bay, 1978.

Cooter, Roger, *The Cultural Meaning of Popular Science: Phrenology and the Organization of Consent in Nineteenth-century Britain*, Cambridge University Press, New York, 1984.

Danalis, John, *Riding the Black Cockatoo* (ebook), Allen & Unwin, 2009

De Giustino, David, *Conquest of Mind: Phrenology and Victorian Social Thought*, Croom Helm, London, 1975.

Dimond, Jill, 'From the Lips of a Lady: Mrs AM Hamilton-Grey's First Biography of Henry Kendall', *Australian Literary Studies*, Vol. 21 (3), 2004, pp. 337–349.

Dimond, Jill, 'Ned Kelly's Skull', Issue 211, *Overland*, 2013.

Douglas, Bronwen and Ballard, Chris (eds), *Foreign Bodies: Oceania and the Science of Race 1750–1940*, ANU Press, Canberra, 2008.

Eades, Diane, *Aboriginal Ways of Using English*, Aboriginal Studies Press, Canberra, 2013.

Enright, Walter John, 'Further Notes on the Worimi', *Mankind*,
Vol. 1 (7), 1933, pp. 161–162.

Faulkhead, Shannon and Berg, Jim (eds), *Power and the Passion: Our
Ancestors Return Home*, Koorie Heritage Trust, Melbourne,
2010.

Fforde, Cressida, *Collecting the Dead*, Duckworth, London, 2004.

Fforde, Cressida, 'From Edinburgh University to the Ngarrindjeri
nation, South Australia', *Museum International*, Vol. 61 (1–2),
2009, pp. 41–47.

Fforde, Cressida, Hubert, Jane and Turnbull, Paul (eds), *The Dead
and Their Possessions: Repatriation in Principle, Policy and Practice*,
Routledge, London, 2002.

Finnane, Mark and Douglas, Heather, *Indigenous Crime and Settler
Law*, Palgrave Macmillan, Houndmills, 2012.

Ford, Reg, *Clarence Town: Erring-I to River Port*, self-published,
Clarence Town, 1987.

Fraser, John, 'The Aborigines of New South Wales',
Proceedings of the Royal Society of New South Wales, Vol. 26,
1882–1883, pp. 193–233.

Frost, Ginger, 'Bigamy and Cohabitation in Victorian England',
Journal of Family History, Vol. 22, 1997, pp. 286–306.

Geller, Pamela L., 'Skeletal Analysis and Theoretical Complications',
World Archaeology, Vol. 37 (4), 2005, pp. 597–609.

Gervasoni, Clare, 'A Confusion of Tongues: overcoming language
difficulties on the Jim Crow Goldfield', in Keir Reeves and
David Nichols (eds), *Deeper Leads: New Approaches to Victorian
Goldfields History*, Ballarat Heritage Services, Ballarat, 2007.

Goodall, Heather, 'New South Wales', in Ann McGrath (ed.),
Contested Ground: Australian Aborigines Under the British Crown,
Allen & Unwin, Sydney, 1995, pp. 55–120.

Goodman, David, 'Fear of Circuses: Founding the National Museum
of Victoria', *Continuum*, Vol. 3 (1), 1990, pp. 18–34.

Goodman, Gail S., 'Children's Testimony in Historical Perspective',
Journal of Social Issues, Vol. 40 (2), 1984, pp. 9–34.

Griffiths, Tom, *Hunters and Collectors: The Antiquarian Imagination in
Australia*, Cambridge University Press, Oakleigh, 1996.

Harman, Kristyn, *Aboriginal Convicts*, UNSW Press, Sydney, 2012.

Harman, Kristyn, 'The Same Measure of Justice: Aboriginal
Convicts in the Australian Penal Colonies', *Australian Studies*,
Vol. 1, 2009, pp. 1–20.

Howitt, Alfred, *Native Tribes of South-East Australia*, The MacMillan Company, New York, 1904.

Hurled Into Eternity: The 16 Executions at Maitland Gaol, Maitland City Council, Maitland, 2012.

Jones, Ross, 'Cadavers and the Social Dimension of Dissection', in Sarah Ferber and Sally Wilde (eds), *The Body Divided: Human Beings and Human 'Material' in Modern Medical History*, Ashgate, Farnham, 2011, pp. 29–52.

Jones, Ross, *Humanity's Mirror: 150 Years of Anatomy in Melbourne*, Haddington Press, South Yarra, 2007.

Kakaliouras, Ann, 'An Anthropology of Repatriation : Contemporary Physical Anthropological and Native American Ontologies of Practice', *Current Anthropology*, Vol. 53 (Supplement 5), 2012, pp. 210–221.

Kaladelfos, Amanda, 'The Politics of Punishment: Rape and the Death Penalty in Colonial Australia, 1841–1901', *History Australia*, Vol. 9 (1), 2012, pp. 155–175.

Kirkup, John, *The Evolution of Surgical Instruments: An Illustrated History from Ancient Times to the Twentieth Century*, Norman Publishing, Novato, 2006.

Knapman, Gareth, 'Resisting Man's Place in Nature: Frederick McCoy's decision to exclude humans from the National Museum of Victoria', Unpublished report, Department of Humanities, Melbourne Museum. Published version to appear in the Historical Records of Australian Science, 2015.

Knudson, Kelly and Stojanowski, Christopher, 'New Directions in Bioarchaeology: Recent Contributions to the Study of Human Social Identities, *Journal of Archaeological Research*, Vol. 16 (4), 2008, pp. 397–432.

Kurin, Danielle, 'Trepanation in South-Central Peru During the Early Late Intermediate Period (ca. AD 1000–1250)', *American Journal of Physical Anthropology*, Vol. 152 (4), 2013, pp. 484–494.

Lundy, John K., 'Physical Anthropology in Forensic Medicine', *Anthropology Today*, Vol. 2(5), 1986, pp. 14–17.

MacDonald, Helen, *Human Remains: Episodes in Human Dissection*, Melbourne University Press, Carlton, 2005.

MacDonald, Helen, *Possessing the Dead*, Melbourne University Press, Carlton, 2010.

McMinn, Winston Gregory, *George Reid*, Melbourne University Press, 1989.

Miller, James, *Koori: A Will to Win*, Angus & Robertson, Sydney, 1985.

Muller, Natalie, 'DNA confirms Ned Kelly's remains', *Australian Geographic*, 1 September 2011. Available at: http://www. australiangeographic.com.au/news/2011/09/dna-confirms-ned-kellys-remains. Accessed 16 May 2014.

Mulvaney, John, *et al.*, *My Dear Spencer: The Letters of FJ Gillen to Baldwin Spencer*, Hyland House, Melbourne, 1997.

Museums Australia, *Continuous Cultures, Ongoing Responsibilities: Principles and Guidelines for Australian museums working with Aboriginal and Torres Strait Islander cultural heritage*, ACT, 2005. Available online through the National Museum of Australia: http://www.nma.gov.au/__data/assets/pdf_file/0020/3296/ ccor_final_feb_05.pdf. Accessed 11 July 2014.

Pardoe, Colin, 'Repatriation, Reburial and Biological Research in Australia: Rhetoric and Practice', in S Tarlow and L Ullman (eds), *Burial Archaeology*, Oxford University Press, Oxford, 2013, pp. 733–761

Pardoe, Colin, 'Report to the Tasmanian Museum and Art Gallery', April 2014, p. 14. Supplied by the author.

Pescott, RTM, *Collections of a Century*, National Museum of Victoria, Melbourne, 1954.

Pickering, Michael, 'Lost in Translation', *Borderlands*, Vol. 7 (2), 2008, pp. 1–18.

Pickering, Michael, 'Where are the Stories?', *The Public Historian*, Vol. 32 (1), 2010, pp. 79–95.

A Pictorial History of Maitland & Morpeth, Compiled and Published by *The Newcastle Herald*, Newcastle, 1996.

Poignant, Roslyn, *Professional Savages*, UNSW Press, Sydney, 2004.

Ramsland, John, *The Rainbow Beach Man: The Life and Times of Les Ridgeway Worimi Elder*, Brolga Publishing, Melbourne, 2009.

Rasmussen, Carolyn, 'Valuable, Practical Information', in Carolyn Rasmussen (ed), *A Museum for the People*, Scribe Publications, 2001.

Reynolds, Henry, 'Aborigines and European Social Hierarchy', *Aboriginal History*, Vol. 7, 1983, pp. 124–133.

Reynolds, Henry, *Frontier*, Allen & Unwin, North Sydney, 1987.

Reynolds, Henry, 'Racial Thought in Early Colonial Australia', *Australian Journal of Politics and History*, Vol. 20, 1974, pp. 45–53.

Reynolds, Henry, *With the White People*, Penguin, Ringwood, 1990.

Robertson, Sarah, 'Sources of bias in the Murray Black Collection: Implications for Paleopathological Analysis', *Australian Aboriginal Studies*, Vol. 1, 2007, pp. 116–130.

Russell, Penny, *A Wish of Distinction*, Melbourne University Press, Carlton, 1994.

Moira Simpson, *Making Representations: Museums in the Post-Colonial Era*, Routledge, London, 1996, p. 237

Smale, Hilary, 'Human Bones Returned for Reburial in Kimberley Community', ABC Online, 30 April 2013. http://www.abc.net.au/local/audio/2013/04/30/3748571.htm. Accessed 5 July 2013.

'St Mary's Hospital', University of Tasmania Archives. Available online: http://www.utas.edu.au/__data/assets/pdf_file/0004/64246/rs_28-St-Marys-Hospital-Hobart-1841-1862.pdf. Accessed 3 March 2014.

Thearle, M. John, 'The Rise and Fall of Phrenology in Australia', *Australian and New Zealand Journal of Psychiatry*, Vol. 27 (3), 1993, pp. 518–525.

Thomas, Martin, 'Because it's your country', Australian Book Review, April 2013. Available online: https://www.australianbookreview.com.au/component/k2/98-april-2013-no-350/1400-because-it-s-your-country. Accessed 20 May 2014.

Turnbull, Paul, 'British Anatomists, Phrenologists and the Construction of the Aboriginal Race, c.1790–1830', *History Compass*, Vol. 5 (1), 2007, pp. 26–50.

Turnbull, Paul, 'The Body and Soul Snatchers', *Eureka Street*, Vol. 7 (7), September 1997, pp. 34–38.

Turnbull, Paul, 'Scientific Theft of Remains in Colonial Australia', *Australian Indigenous Law Review*, Vol. 11 (1), 2007, pp. 92–102.

Van Wyhe, John, 'The Diffusion of Phrenology', in *Science in the Marketplace*, Aileen Fyfe and Bernard Lightman (eds), University of Chicago Press, 2007, pp 60–93.

Van Wyhe, John, *Phrenology and the Origins of Victorian Scientific Naturalism*, Ashgate, Aldershot, 2004.

Van Wyhe, John, 'Was phrenology a reform science? Towards a new generalization for phrenology', *History of Science*, Vol. xlii, 2004, pp. 313–331.

Waddell, James, *A History of St Peter's Church, East Maitland, NSW*, Maitland, 1996.

Wafer, Jim and Lissarague, Amanda, *A Handbook of Aboriginal Languages*, Nambucca Heads, 2008.

Waterhouse, Richard, 'The Internationalisation of American Popular Culture in the Nineteenth Century: The Case of the Minstrel Show', *Australasian Journal of American Studies*, Vol. 4 (1), 1985, pp. 1–11.

Wilkinson, Ian, 'The Battle for the Museum: Frederick McCoy and the Establishment of the National Museum of Victoria at the University of Melbourne', *Historical Records of Australian Science*, Vol. 11 (1), 1996, p. 1–11.

Whitman, CO (ed.), 'Microscopy', *The American Naturalist*, Vol. 20 (4), 1886, pp. 406–407

Williams, Michael, 'Aboriginal people – the Gringai', History in the Williams River Valley website. http://williamsvalleyhistory.org.

Wilson, Dean, 'Explaining the "Criminal" Ned Kelly's Death Mask', *The La Trobe Journal*, No. 69, 2002, pp. 51–58.

Wilson, Janice Evelyn, 'Signs of the Mind: Science, Psychological Knowledge and Social Hegemony in Colonial Australia', PhD Thesis, University of Western Australia, 1994, Microfiche mc G 6631, National Library of Australia.

Wood, Marilyn, 'Nineteenth Century Bureaucratic Construction of Indigenous Identities in New South Wales', in Peterson, Nicolas and Sanders, Will (eds), *Citizenship and Indigenous Australians*, Cambridge University Press, Oakleigh, 1998.

Websites

Australian Historic Shipwreck Preservation Project: www.ahspp.org.au

Australian War Memorial: http://www.awm.gov.au/encyclopedia/vietnam_mia/

Design & Art Australia Online: www.dao.org

Gazetteer of Australian Place Names, Geoscience Australia: www.ga/gov.au/place-name

Measuring Worth: www.measuringworth.com

Intersex Society of North America: www.isna.org

'The Landsborough List':
  http://www.ayrshireroots.com/Genealogy/Records/
  Census/1820s/Landsborough/November%201819%20G-H.htm
Organisation Intersex International Australia: oii.org.au
Williams River Valley History: williamsvalleyhistory.org

Acknowledgments

I was able to develop this project to its fullest potential thanks to the assistance of numerous people whom I met while searching for Jim Crow.

I have been fortunate to benefit from the mentorship and expertise of two leading Australian historians. Professor Bain Attwood was my supervisor for the thesis component of my Postgraduate Diploma in Arts (Research) at Monash University, and shared his immense knowledge on Aboriginal–settler relations in the nineteenth century, while offering valuable advice on everything from secondary sources to structure and style. At the Australian National University, my PhD supervisor, Professor Tom Griffiths, has supported me in the delicate task of expanding this manuscript into a book; to work with Tom is as much about becoming a better historian as it is to undertake an apprenticeship in the craft of writing.

I am also very grateful to Associate Professor Martin Thomas for advising me on several drafts of my manuscript and on particular points of anthropological history, and to Dr Gareth Knapman for allowing me to refer to an unpublished version of his paper on Frederick McCoy.

At Museum Victoria, I was generously supported by Rob McWilliams, Valerie Brown, Antoinette Smith, Melanie Raberts, Lindy Allen, Mary Morris and Dr Philip Batty. Some of my most exciting days were spent in the visiting researcher room of the Humanities Department, and it was a privilege to return half a year later as a research assistant, working alongside Rob and learning from his repatriation expertise. The Museum also awarded me an 1854 Student Scholarship that funded my research trip to Sydney and Maitland.

I am very grateful for the subject area expertise of Dr Amanda Kaladelfos on nineteenth-century depositions, and of Dr Michael Williams on the Williams River Valley. Dr Gary Presland and Helen Harris advised me on the Public Records Office of Victoria and the history of Victoria Police for my initial project, which took a side step to become the search for Jim Crow. Helen has also been a sounding board for all things marital and divorce (in the historical sense, of course), as has Professor Angela Woollacott. Dr Colin Pardoe was very kind in advising me in the niche area of physical anthropology.

Malcolm Osborn at the Geological Survey of New South Wales assisted me by confirming the location of the diminutive Boat Fall Creek, enabling me to draw conclusions about the Boatfall Tribe in the blanket lists of the 1830s. Dan Harrison kindly introduced me to the short stories of Henry Lawson.

The archivists and librarians at the State Library of Victoria, Public Records Office of Victoria, Mitchell Library, NSW State Records and Prahran Mechanics' Institute Victorian History Library were invariably knowledgeable, putting me in touch with materials that became fundamental to this book. The enthusiasm of Belinda Borg, archivist at Museum Victoria, was truly infectious on the afternoon we spent trawling through the papers related to the Industrial and Technological Museum.

The curious tides of historical thought mean that AS Hamilton has also recently piqued the interest of another researcher, Jill Dimond, whose paper explaining her theory that Hamilton collected Ned Kelly's skull was published in winter 2013 in *Overland*. While I have referred at various points to Jill's 2004 paper on Agnes Hamilton-Grey, and am grateful for the *Overland* piece in pointing me towards the Hamilton divorce file in the Hobart archives, almost all of my research on the phrenologist himself was completed in early 2013, and I did not become aware of the *Overland* paper until the week before my thesis was due for submission in October 2013.

Finally, I could not have completed this work without the love and care of my family – my parents Hubert and Jadwiga and my brilliant sister Maz.

Index